Campgrounds of Santa Barbara and Ventura Counties

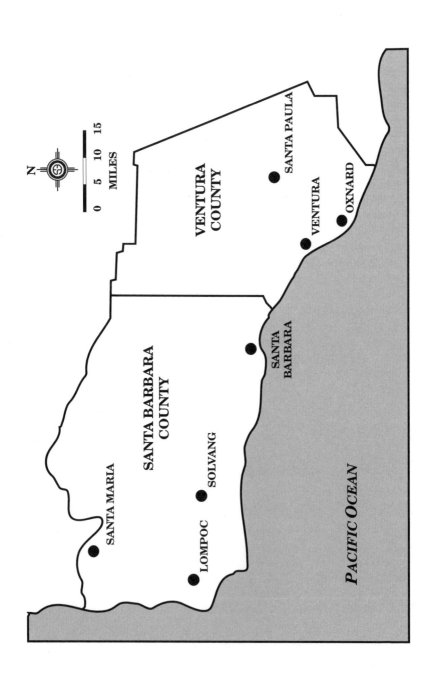

Campgrounds of Santa Barbara and Ventura Counties

Jeff Tyler

Sunbelt Guidebooks and Maps
"Natural Adventures in the Californias"
A series edited by Lowell Lindsay

SUNBELT PUBLICATIONS
San Diego, California

Edited by Laurie Gibson
Book design and composition by W. G. Hample & Associates
Project Management by Joni Harlan
Cover design by Leah Cooper
Printed in the United States of America

Sunbelt Publications, Inc.
P.O. Box 191126
San Diego, CA 92159-1126
(935) 258-4911 (935) 258-4916 fax (area code 619 until June 2000)
www.sunbeltpub.com

04 03 02 01 00   5 4 3 2 1

Library of Congress Cataloging-in-Publication Data

Tyler, Jeff H.
    Campgrounds of Santa Barbara and Ventura Counties/Jeff Tyler.
    –1st ed. p.cm
    Includes index,
    ISBN 0-932653-36-7
    1. Camp sites, facilities, etc.–Santa Barbara County–Directories. 2.
Camp sites, facilities, etc.–California–Ventura County–Directories. 3.
Santa Barbara County (Calif.)–Guidebooks. 4. Ventura County (Calif.)–
Guidebooks. I. Title.

GV191.42.C2 T95 2000
646'947949109'025–dc21

                                                          00-035788

All photos by Jeff Tyler unless otherwise noted.
Cover photo: Digital imagery copyright 1999 PhotoDisk, Inc.

Contents

Preface

I first tried camping out at the age of eleven. I purchased a tent from a neighbor and pitched it in a far corner of the backyard. With permission from my mother, I set out to savor sleeping "in the cool of the night among the night sounds." Three things quickly became apparent. The night sounds of Los Angeles are quite the same as its day sounds. Second, California nights do cool down, and though I had blankets, I was still cold. Finally, secondhand canvas is not necessarily waterproof. It was a long dash through the mud to the back porch, in the middle of the night, with arms full of bedding, in the pouring rain.

In later years, in spite of heckling from rugged tent-camping buddies of mine, I bought a 23-foot RV. Although it had its problems, at least the roof stayed in place. However, with the help of low-lying tree limbs, it too developed leaks. Today, for backcountry outings (when my wife isn't on board), I stick to a four-wheel-drive pickup with a low-profile camper shell.

Campgrounds of Santa Barbara and Ventura Counties contains up-to-date, field-checked information on the public campgrounds in Santa Barbara and Ventura Counties. Whether you're planning to camp in the comforts of your RV or in a tent pulled from the trunk of your car, this book contains all the information you'll need for your next camping adventure.

The first part of the book describes campgrounds in Santa Barbara County, and the second part, campgrounds in Ventura County. Within each part, the campground descriptions are grouped together for each county by location: coastal area, inland valley area, and mountain area. Within each area, campgrounds have been assigned numbers that correspond to a map showing the general location of each. The descriptions contain information on the general setting and features of each campground; fees, restrictions, number of sites, and contact information; and directions for getting there. The appendixes include a directory of useful phone numbers and addresses and information on Adventure Passes and critters you might encounter while camping.

Campground conditions can change rapidly—storm and fire damage, damage to access roads, budget constraints, and closings to protect sensitive habitats can all affect a campground. In addition, campgrounds often fill up quickly during the summer months.

When in doubt, contact the agency having jurisdiction over the campground before making the trip.

I've tried to provide accurate information, but if you find, after visiting a campground, that I've overlooked important features, I welcome your comments.

Jeff Tyler
April 2000

Santa Barbara County

Santa Barbara County has some of the finest public campgrounds in the California State Park and U.S. Forest Service systems. The county also has one of the longest coastlines in California—over 100 miles. The coast boasts four large state campgrounds and one county park, which provide excellent camping opportunities with ocean access.

The mountains in the county are part of the Transverse Range, the only major range of mountains in the two American continents that runs east and west rather than north and south. Elevations seldom exceed 5000 feet, and the mountain ridges of the coastal Santa Ynez Mountains and the backcountry San Rafael Mountains are often separated by beautiful, small valleys that run parallel to the ridges. Camping facilities are good, with accommodations ranging from the standard tent and RV sites to yurts (yurts are American simulations of the tent-like abodes found in Mongolia; see Cachuma Lake Recreation Area).

The county abounds in places to see: Vandenberg Air Force Base, the Danish village of Solvang and the city of Santa Barbara with its specialty shops and historic buildings. Buellton boasts the very first Andersen's Pea Soup Restaurant. Gaviota Pass is the extremely narrow pass where in 1846 Californios waited to ambush Colonel John C. Fremont U.S.A. and his battalion. He went over San Marcos Pass instead, and in so doing captured the town of Santa Barbara without bloodshed. The county has three missions, which makes it first in number of missions—Santa Barbara Mission in the city of Santa Barbara, La Purisima Concepcion (The Immaculate Conception) at Lompoc, and Santa Ines.

For those who want to get away from it all, amidst beautiful surroundings and a pleasant climate, Santa Barbara County's campgrounds are hard to beat.

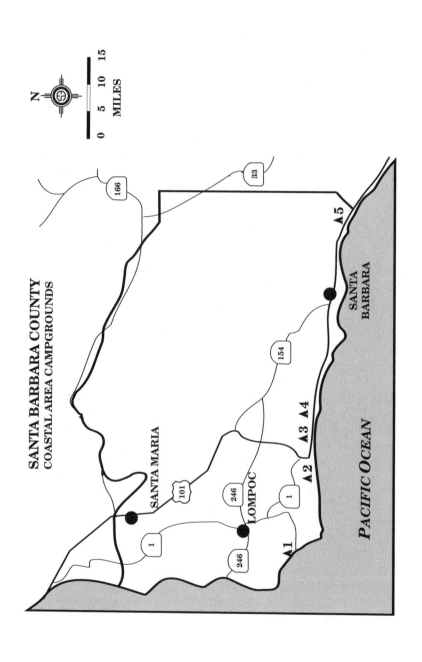

SANTA BARBARA COUNTY
COASTAL AREA CAMPGROUNDS

N

0   5   10   15
MILES

166

33

SANTA MARIA

101

246

1

246

LOMPOC

1

A1

A2

A3 A4

154

SANTA
BARBARA

A5

PACIFIC OCEAN

SANTA BARBARA COUNTY COASTAL AREA

▲1 Jalama Beach County Park
　　Gaviota Rest Area
▲2 Gaviota State Park
▲3 Refugio State Beach
▲4 El Capitan State Beach

▲5 Carpinteria State Beach
　　Santa Rosa
　　San Miguel
　　Santa Cruz
　　Anacapa

Jalama Beach County Park

3

Jalama Beach County Park
Santa Barbara County Parks

GENERAL SETTING (LOCATION, FEATURES, SUPPLIES, IN-FORMATION) This coastal county park is located on a small, remote bay between Point Conception and Point Arguello, southwest of Lompoc where the Santa Ynez Mountains meet the sea. A cool, marine climate prevails most of the year, and fog frequently rolls in, giving the coast an unworldly appearance. Monterey cypress trees and coastal live oaks dot the landscape. An occasional train, passing along the trestle east of the park, pierces the quiet. Near Jalama Creek is the site of an ancient village of Chumash Native Americans who were lured by the pleasant climate and the oaks' plentiful acorns. Some sites sit on a bluff, above the rest of camp, with a view of the ocean. The ocean is easily seen from the beach picnic area and appears turquoise on clear, sunny days.

Visit La Purisima Mission State Historic Park with Mission La Purisima Concepcion (The Immaculate Conception) near Lompoc. California's charming "Little Denmark," the village of Solvang, is roughly 34 miles east, via Highway 246. Vandenberg Air Force Base, north of Lompoc, offers tours; reservations are required.

Beach recreation includes surfing and swimming. *Caution:* there is no lifeguard and the water is very cold. Fishing brings in perch, halibut, and kelp bass (license required). The park features two playgrounds, a basketball court, horseshoe pits, and three picnic areas, one along the beach and two inland (see next page for facilities). A ranger resides at the park's northeast corner.

Gasoline and supplies are available in Lompoc, 20 miles northwest. The park's store, at the north side, carries limited supplies, groceries, ice, firewood, bait, and tackle. For more information, phone the park or write Santa Barbara County Parks Department.

SITES, FEES, FACILITIES, RESTRICTIONS There are 110 nonreservable, individual sites. Of these, 29 sites are for RVs and have electrical hookups, and the nightly fee is $21 per site ($18 for senior citizens). The other 81 sites, for tents or RVs, have no hookups, and the nightly fee is $15 per site ($13 for senior citizens). Up to eight people and two vehicles are allowed at each individual site. The nightly fee for the second vehicle is $8. Special weekly rates are available during fall and winter; phone for details. Each site has a picnic table and a steel fire ring with grill.

There are three group camping areas for tents or RVs: Areas A, B, and D. The fee at Area A (no hookups), with a limit of seven vehicles, is $84 nightly. The fee at Area B (electrical hookups), with a limit of 13 vehicles, is $273 nightly. Areas A and B are reservable, September 15 to March 31, only. Area D (no hookups) is reservable all year, with a limit of eight vehicles, for $96 nightly. Reservations are available for a nonrefundable fee of $25.

Each group site has several picnic tables and some or all of the following: a preparation table, a sink, a pedestal barbecue, a large concrete barbecue, and a concrete fire ring without grill.

Other facilities include piped water spigots, four restrooms with sinks and flush toilets, a hot-shower facility and RV dump station (both near the entrance), pay phones at the entrance and at the north side near the ranger's residence, and trash cans.

Wheelchair access is provided at restrooms, at one of the showers, and at some sites that have level, paved spurs.

Each picnic area has picnic tables and room for parking. One picnic area has pedestal barbecues also. The day-use fee is $5 per vehicle. Day-use hours are from 9 A.M. until dusk.

The park is usually open, but at times is subject to closure due to nearby Vandenberg Air Force Base operations. Camping limit is 14 days. Check-out is at 2 P.M. Quiet time is from 10 P.M. to 8 A.M. Anyone 17 years of age or under must be accompanied by an adult. Fires are permitted only in the park's barbecues and fire rings. No plants, animals, wood, rocks, or any other natural features may be removed, since all are protected by law. Dogs must be leashed; the nightly fee or day-use fee is $2 per dog. Owners must clean up after their pets.

DIRECTIONS From central Santa Barbara, take U.S. Highway 101 northwest about 26 miles to State Highway 1 (1.5 miles beyond Gaviota Tunnel and Gaviota Pass). Turn left (west) and go about 13.5 miles to Jalama Road. Turn left (south) and go about 14 miles to the coast and the park entrance station.

Gaviota Rest Area

This CALTRANS rest area is located nearly midway between Santa Barbara and Santa Maria and is about a mile north of Gaviota State Park and the ocean. No camping is allowed. Facilities include picnic tables, pay phones, newspaper vending machines, information boards, drinking fountains, restrooms with sinks and flush toilets, trash cans, and a pet area. Restrooms and paved pathways are wheelchair accessible. Dogs must be leashed.

The rest area is off U.S. Highway 101, about 33.5 miles west of central Santa Barbara. It is just north of where Highway 101 leaves the coast and turns inland, and is south of Gaviota Tunnel.

Gaviota State Park

GENERAL SETTING (LOCATION, FEATURES, SUPPLIES, INFORMATION) *Gaviota* is a common and appropriate name around this region. It is a Spanish word that means *seagull*, a bird we associate with the beach. Besides being the name of this state park, Gaviota is the name of a creek, peak, pass, spring, tunnel, rest area, and a tiny coastal crossroad with a fire station.

Gaviota State Park comprises nearly 2800 acres, in the coastal hills surrounding Gaviota Pass, and is about 33 miles west of Santa Barbara. The campground sits at the mouth of a canyon, Cañada de la Gaviota, between the beach and Gaviota Creek. The camp is visually separated from the beach by the trestle of the coastal railroad. Though the camp is unshaded, it has a few bushes. The ocean view and nearby eucalyptus trees add a touch of beauty. Kids get a kick out of watching trains go across the trestle.

Special features include a fishing pier and boat launch hoist (limit three tons). Fishing requires a license, except on the pier. Swimmers are cautioned that lifeguard service is provided only during summer. The park has a picnic area along the beach (with picnic tables), a hiking trail, and a day-use parking lot. At times a camp host is present to answer questions and be of assistance.

Solvang, the village with a Danish theme, is near the old mission with a Spanish theme. Both are located within the Santa Ynez Valley. From Gaviota State Beach, take Highway 101 about 11 miles north to Buellton, then Highway 246 about 3 miles east to Solvang. The mission is situated at the eastern edge of Solvang.

Supplies are available in Buellton, about 11 miles north, via U.S. Highway 101. The park store is open in the summer and carries groceries, ice, firewood, and bait. The camp host sells firewood. For more information, write or phone Gaviota State Park.

SITES, FEES, FACILITIES, RESTRICTIONS The park has 52 nonreservable, numbered sites for tents or RVs (no hookups), with up to eight people per site. During summer, arrive at 7 A.M. to get on the campsite waiting list. Fees per site, per night, follow. On

Friday or Saturday night, year-round, the fee is $16. On other nights, the fee is $15 from March 16 through November, and is $14 otherwise. The day-use fee is $5 per vehicle. Sites have black-top spurs. Most sites and all restrooms are wheelchair accessible. Each site has a picnic table and a steel fire ring with grill. The park has restrooms with sinks, hot (pay) showers, and flush toilets. There are drinking fountains, a pay phone, a newspaper vending machine, information boards, dumpsters, and trash cans. Registered campers may use the RV water and dump stations at El Capitan State Beach, 12 miles east, via U.S. Highway 101.

The park is usually open, but is subject to closure during rainy weather. Camping limit is 7 days, June to September, and 15 days, October to May. Check-out is at 12 noon. Quiet time is from 10 P.M. to 6 A.M. Maximum length for trailers is 25 feet, and for motorhomes and campers, 27 feet. Fires are permitted only in the park's fire rings. Dogs must be leashed and kept away from the beach, creek area, and trails. The nightly fee is $1 per dog.

DIRECTIONS From central Santa Barbara, take U.S. Highway 101 west about 33 miles to Gaviota Beach Road. Turn left (south), and go about a quarter mile to the entrance (follow the signs).

Refugio State Beach

GENERAL SETTING (LOCATION, FEATURES, SUPPLIES, INFORMATION) On a clear day, the Channel Islands are visible from this state beach. Santa Rosa Island lies directly south, and Santa Cruz Island lies southeast. A few campsites near the beach have the best views of the ocean and the islands. Much of the camping area is shaded by eucalyptus trees and palms.

This 155-acre state beach is located west of Santa Barbara, and the elevation is sea level. You can swim, surf, or fish (license required). *Caution:* a lifeguard is on duty only during summer. A picnic area, playground, campfire center, and hiking and bicycling trails are provided. The camp host, at Site 44, sells firewood.

Local attractions to visit include Mission Santa Barbara, Santa Barbara Zoological Gardens, Sea Center aquariums at Santa Barbara Harbor, and South Coast Railroad Museum in Goleta.

Supplies and gasoline are available in Goleta, about 15 miles east, via U.S. Highway 101. The state beach store, open during summer, carries limited supplies. For additional information, contact Refugio State Beach.

SITES, FEES, FACILITIES, RESTRICTIONS The state beach has 85 individual, numbered sites (no hookups). Nightly fees, per site, follow. From April 1 to October 31, the fee is $18 on Friday and Saturday, and $17 on other nights. From November 1 to March 31, the fee is $15 on every night. Up to eight people and three vehicles are allowed at each site. The nightly fee for the second and third vehicles is $5 per vehicle. Sites and spurs are made of gravel, and camp roads are paved.

Each individual site has a picnic table and a steel fire ring (with grill) or a pedestal barbecue.

There is one developed group site, which accommodates up to 80 people and 25 vehicles (including trailers), for $120 a night. This group site has picnic tables and steel fire rings with grills.

Reservations for all campsites are recommended from March 15 to November 30, and are $7.50 per site.

The campground has wheelchair-accessible restrooms with sinks, hot (pay) showers, and flush toilets. Drinking fountains, dumpsters, and trash cans are provided. Pay phones are located at the entrance and beach store. Registered campers may use the RV water station and RV dump station at El Capitan State Beach, about 3 miles east, via U.S. Highway 101.

The small, primitive, hike and bike camping area, for tents, is close to the beach; the nightly fee is $3 per person. The day-use parking area is located between the campground and the beach, and the day-use parking fee is $5 per vehicle.

Refugio State Beach is open throughout the year, but is subject to closure during rainy weather. Camping limit at individual campsites is 7 days, June to September, and 15 days, October to May. Camping limit at the group site is seven days, year-round. Check-out is at 12 noon. Quiet hours are from 10 P.M. to 6 A.M. Maximum length for trailers is 27 feet, and for motorhomes and campers, 30 feet. Fires are restricted to the state beach's barbecues and fire rings. Dogs must be leashed; they are not allowed on the beach or on trails. The nightly fee is $1 per dog.

DIRECTIONS From central Santa Barbara, take U.S. Highway 101 west about 23 miles to Refugio Road. Exit the freeway, turn left (south), and go under the freeway, toward the ocean, to the entrance station.

El Capitan State Beach

GENERAL SETTING (LOCATION, FEATURES, SUPPLIES, INFORMATION) The Channel Islands silhouetted against a sunset of orange and pink are one of the many reasons why visitors enjoy staying here. The protruding coastline affords a wide view of the ocean and coastline. Coastal scrub oaks, sycamores, and pepper trees partially shade various parts of the campground. The state beach contains 133 acres and sits at an elevation of 10 feet.

Surfing, swimming, and surf fishing (license required) are popular here. *Caution:* a lifeguard is on duty only during summer. Featured are a beach picnic area with picnic tables and barbecues, a campfire center (amphitheater), nature trails, and a bicycle path. The camp host resides at Campsite 42 and sells firewood.

Local points of interest include Mission Santa Barbara, Sea Center's aquariums at Santa Barbara Harbor, Santa Barbara Zoological Gardens, and South Coast Railroad Museum in Goleta.

Supplies are available in Goleta, about 12 miles east, via U.S. Highway 101. The state beach store, open during summer, carries limited supplies, groceries, ice, firewood, and bait. For more information, write El Capitan State Beach.

SITES, FEES, FACILITIES, RESTRICTIONS There are 140 individual, numbered sites for tents and RVs (no hookups). Fees, per site, per night, are as follows. From April 1 to October 31, the fee is $18 on Friday and Saturday, and $17 on other nights. From November 1 to March 31, the fee is $15 on every night. Up to eight persons and three vehicles are allowed at each site. The nightly fee for the second and third vehicles is $5 per vehicle.

Each individual site has a picnic table and a steel fire ring with grill. The state beach has blacktop parking spurs and blacktop sites. Some sites and restrooms are wheelchair accessible.

There are three group sites for tents (not RVs). *Drake* site takes up to 125 people and 25 vehicles for $187.50 nightly. *Cabrillo* site takes up to 75 people and 15 vehicles for $112.50 nightly. *Ortega* site takes up to 50 people and 10 vehicles for $75 nightly.

One group site is for self-contained RVs (not tents). *Del Mar* site takes up to 100 people and 25 vehicles for $120 nightly. It sits on a low bluff, with an ocean view, and has an RV parking area.

Each group site has picnic tables and some or all of the following: a pedestal barbecue, a steel fire ring (with grill), a concrete fire ring (without grill), and a sink with attached service table.

Restrooms have sinks, hot (pay) showers, and flush toilets; some also have dressing rooms and outdoor laundry sinks. Dumpsters and trash cans are provided. Pay phones are available at the entrance, the store, Ortega group site, and near Site 128. An RV potable water station and dump station are available.

Reservations are recommended and are $7.50 per site. The hike and bike camping area, near the group camping area, can be accessed by the bike path. It has four primitive tent sites; the nightly fee is $3 per person. The day-use parking area is between the campground and the beach; the day-use fee is $5 per vehicle.

The state beach is usually open, but is subject to closure during rainy weather. Camping limit at individual sites is 7 days, June to September, and 15 days, October to May. Limit at group sites is seven days, year-round. Check-out is at 12 noon. Quiet time is from 10 P.M. to 6 A.M. Maximum length for trailers is 27 feet, and for motorhomes and campers, 30 feet. Fires are permitted only in the state beach's barbecues and fire rings. Dogs must be leashed. The nightly fee is $1 per dog.

DIRECTIONS From central Santa Barbara, take U.S. Highway 101 west about 20 miles to the El Capitan Beach exit. Exit, turn left (south), and go under the freeway, toward the ocean, about a quarter mile to the entrance station.

Carpinteria State Beach
Santa Rosa, San Miguel, Santa Cruz, and Anacapa Campgrounds

GENERAL SETTING (LOCATION, FEATURES, SUPPLIES, INFORMATION) Carpinteria State Beach is the best equipped of the state beaches in Santa Barbara County and has the most campsites, numbering over 250. These sites are divided among four neighboring campgrounds that are named for the local Channel Islands: Santa Rosa, San Miguel, Santa Cruz, and Anacapa. The state beach contains 84 acres, and the elevation ranges from 0 to 20 feet. Signs direct you around the state beach and campgrounds. Each campground has a resident host that sells firewood.

Short pines and umbrella-shaped myoprom trees predominate throughout the state beach and campgrounds, and some sites, such as those at Santa Rosa Camp, have been placed in eucalyptus groves. The picnic area, near the main entrance, is separated from the beach by a sand dune. There is a sand volleyball court, a campfire center, a playground, and a visitor center (open limited hours). Some of the local museums contain displays of objects from the American pioneer era and artifacts from the Chumash Native American era. Carpinteria Valley Museum is located on Maple Avenue, a few blocks north of the state beach. Two museums are located in downtown Santa Barbara, about 10 miles west of Carpinteria: Santa Barbara Historical Museum and Santa Barbara Museum of Art. Santa Barbara has one of the most beautiful of California's missions, and Santa Barbara Museum of Natural History is near the mission. At Santa Barbara Harbor, Sea Center's aquariums house local marine life. Santa Barbara Zoological Gardens includes a variety of animals, birds, and plants.

The Pacific Ocean offers swimming and surf fishing (license required). *Caution:* lifeguards are on duty only during summer.

Supplies are available in Carpinteria and at the state beach's store, open during summer. For additional information, write or phone Carpinteria State Beach.

SITES, FEES, FACILITIES, RESTRICTIONS Individual (family) sites are numbered and divided among four camps. There are 86 full-hookup sites, 34 partial-hookup sites (with electricity and water), and 140 non-hookup sites. (Five sites are occupied by camp hosts.) There are also two group camping sections, open seasonally, one at Santa Cruz Camp, and the other at Anacapa Camp. Each group section consists of several adjacent individual campsites.

Camping fees per site, per night, with maximum lengths for RVs, and with tent status (in parentheses), are listed below. RVs include motorhomes, trailers, and campers. These fees include one vehicle and eight people per site. Each additional vehicle must be parked in the parking lot, for a nightly fee of $5 per vehicle.

Santa Rosa Campground. This camp has 86 full-hookup sites divided among the following sections:
Beach Row Section
This section has 25 full-hookup sites. From March 15 to September 30, the fee is $29 on Friday and Saturday, and $28 on other nights. From October 1 to March 14, the fee is $25 on every night. Allowable RV length is 24 feet (one small tent permitted).
Long Row and Inland Sections
These sections have 20 and 41 full-hookup sites, respectively. From March 15 to September 30, the fee is $24 on Friday and Saturday,

and $23 on other nights. From October 1 to March 14, the fee is $20 on every night. Long Row allowable RV length is 30 feet (no tents). Inland RV length is 24 feet at some sites (with one small tent), and 21 feet at other sites (no tents).

San Miguel Campground. There are 33 partial-hookup sites and 40 non-hookup sites divided among the following sections:

Long Row and Inland Sections

Each of these sections has 17 partial-hookup sites (total of 34 sites). From March 15 to September 30, the fee is $24 on Friday and Saturday, and $23 on other nights. From October 1 to March 14, the fee is $20 on every night. Long Row allowable RV length is 30 feet (no tents). Inland RV length is 21 feet (no tents).

Beach Row Section

This section has 18 non-hookup sites. From March 15 to September 30, the fee is $23 on Friday and Saturday, and $22 on other nights. From October 1 to March 14, the fee is $19 on every night. Allowable RV length is 24 feet (one small tent permitted).

Inland Section

There are 22 non-hookup sites. From March 15 to September 30, the fee is $18 on Friday and Saturday, and $17 on other nights. From October 1 to March 14, the fee is $14 on every night. Allowable RV length is 21 feet (one small tent for two people permitted).

Santa Cruz and Anacapa Campgrounds. The camps have 61 and 39 individual, non-hookup sites, respectively, for RVs (some are suitable for tents). Sites are divided according to RV lengths.

Individual sites with maximum RV lengths of 35 feet. From March 15 to September 30, the fee is $18 on Friday and Saturday, and $18 on other nights. From October 1 to March 14, the fee is $14 on every night.

Individual sites with maximum RV lengths of 28 feet. From March 15 to September 30, the fee is $18 on Friday and Saturday, and $17 on other nights. From October 1 to March 14, the fee is $14 on every night.

Santa Cruz Campground's Group Section

This section consists of eight individual sites and accommodates a maximum of 64 people and eight vehicles for $150 per night. The section has no hookups, and the maximum RV length is 35 feet.

Anacapa Campground's Group Section

This group section consists of five individual sites and accommodates a maximum of 40 people and five vehicles. The fee is $100 per night. This group section has no hookups, and the maximum RV length is 35 feet.

Reservations are required for all campsites at all four Carpinteria State Beach campgrounds and are $7.50 per site. Each individual (family) site has a picnic table and a steel fire ring (with grill) or a pedestal barbecue. Group camping sections, being grouped individual campsites, have picnic tables and steel fire rings (with grills). Many campsites have blacktop spurs and some are wheelchair accessible, as are restrooms.

Campgrounds have restrooms with sinks, hot (pay) showers, and flush toilets. Some restrooms have outdoor laundry sinks. Outdoor showers are also provided to wash off sand and salt water. An RV water station and dump station are located near the entrance. Other facilities include drinking fountains, information boards, dumpsters, trash cans, and newspaper vending machines (near the store). Pay telephones are located near the entrance and at restrooms in Santa Rosa and San Miguel campgrounds.

The hike and bike camp, near Anacapa Campground, has four primitive tent sites; the nightly fee is $3 per person.

The picnic area has two large picnic sites, suitable for groups. Each picnic site has 16 picnic tables, two large pedestal barbecues, and a large picnic shelter (shade ramada). The picnic area has two restrooms, one at each picnic site, with sinks and flush toilets. Outdoor showers are provided to wash off sand and salt water. Drinking fountains, trash cans, and a day-use parking area are also provided. The day-use fee is $5 per vehicle.

The state beach is usually open, but is subject to closure during rainy weather. At individual sites, the camping limit is 7 days, June to September, and 15 days, October to May. Group sites are available from March 15 to September 30, and the camping limit is 7 days. Check-in is at 2 P.M.; check-out is at 12 noon. Quiet time is from 10 P.M. to 6 A.M. The juvenile curfew of 8:30 P.M. is enforced for anyone who is 17 years of age or younger. For fires, use only the state beach's barbecues and fire rings. Dogs must be leashed and are not allowed on the beach. The nightly fee is $1 per dog.

DIRECTIONS From central Santa Barbara, take U.S. Highway 101 about 11 miles southeast to Casitas Pass Road in Carpinteria. Exit, turn right, and go a quarter mile to Carpinteria Avenue. Turn right, and go a quarter mile to Palm Avenue. Turn left, and go about half a mile to the entrance station.

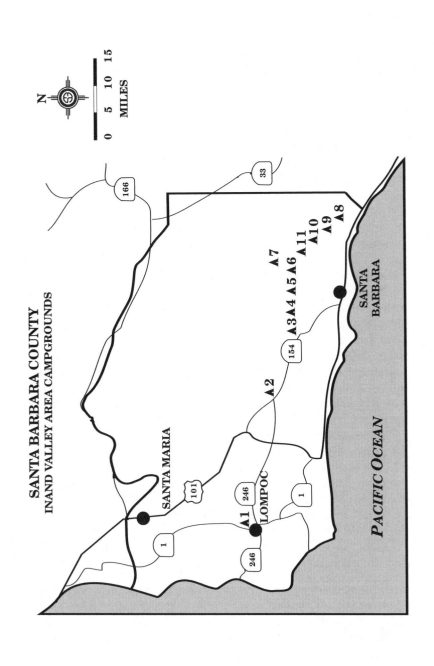

SANTA BARBARA COUNTY
INAND VALLEY AREA CAMPGROUNDS

SANTA BARBARA COUNTY
INLAND VALLEY AREA

▲ 1 River Park
▲ 2 Cachuma Lake Recreation
       Area
▲ 3 Fremont
▲ 4 Paradise
▲ 5 Los Prietos

▲ 6 Sage Hill Group
▲ 7 Upper Oso
▲ 8 Juncal
▲ 9 Middle Santa Ynez
▲10 P-Bar Flats
▲11 Mono

Mono Campground

River Park
Lompoc Parks and Recreation

GENERAL SETTING (LOCATION, FEATURES, SUPPLIES, INFORMATION) A memorial to veterans of the war in Vietnam, placed at the rear of this park, is a distinguishing feature. An outdoor display of historical farm equipment used in the Lompoc Valley, described by signs, forms a mini-museum along the east side of the park's road, opposite the RV camping area and next to agricultural fields. A little lake and its fountain are the focal point of the picnic and group camping areas. The lake has a nice view of the surrounding valley and agricultural fields. The RV area is shaded by liquid amber trees. The picnic and group camping areas are shaded by oaks, small pines, and cedars. River Park is owned and operated by the City of Lompoc, and is located just east of the city.

Tours of Vandenberg Air Force Base, a major aerospace facility north of Lompoc, are offered; reservations are required. La Purisima Mission State Historic Park is located about 3 miles northeast of Lompoc, and Solvang, California's colorful little Danish capital, is 21 miles west of Lompoc. The annual Lompoc Flower Festival is held on the last weekend in June, complete with a parade and marching bands, a carnival and booths, and self-guided tours of the flower fields; contact Lompoc Valley Chamber of Commerce. The Lompoc Museum contains Chumash artifacts.

The park has a playground, volleyball courts, horseshoe pits, an exercise path, and a picnic area with tables, barbecues, and drinking fountains. The lake is stocked with fish; fishing requires a license. A park ranger and a resident camp host are in the park.

Supplies are available nearby in Lompoc. For further information, contact Lompoc Parks and Recreation Department.

SITES, FEES, FACILITIES, RESTRICTIONS The park's individual and family camping area has 36 nonreservable, numbered RV campsites with full hookups. The nightly fee, $15 per site, includes one vehicle and a limit of eight people per site. No more than two vehicles are allowed per site, and the nightly fee for the second vehicle is $10. Phone for weekly rates. Each of these sites has a picnic table, a steel fire ring with grill, and a water spigot.

The group camping area has five group sites. Phone for group arrangements, fees, and reservations. Each group site has a large concrete barbecue, several picnic tables, a preparation table, a large gazebo (shelter), and a water spigot. The group area has parking lots that include wheelchair parking spaces.

Both camping areas have restrooms with sinks, flush toilets, hot showers, and wheelchair access. There is an RV dump station, for which a day-use fee of $2 is charged if you are not registered in camp. Other facilities include drinking fountains, trash cans, pay phones, and newspaper vending machines.

The park is usually open. Camping limit is 14 days, May 1 to September 30, and 30 days, October 1 to April 30. Check-out is at 2 P.M. Quiet hours are from 10 P.M. to 7 A.M. An adult must accompany a youth under 18 years of age. No swimming or wading is permitted in the lake. Motorized cycles are only permitted on paved roadways and in parking lots. Maximum RV length is 34 feet. For fires, use only the park's fire rings and fire pits. Nearby riverbed wood may be gathered, but other vegetation and wildlife are protected. Pets must be leashed, kept 50 feet away from the lake, and owners must clean up after them. The nightly fee is $1 per pet.

DIRECTIONS From U.S. Highway 101 in Buellton, take State Highway 246 west about 16 miles to the River Park entrance (opposite Sweeney Road). Turn right (north) and enter the park.

Cachuma Lake Recreation Area
Santa Barbara County Parks

GENERAL SETTING (LOCATION, FEATURES, SUPPLIES, INFORMATION) Solvang and Santa Ynez lie to the west of this favorite recreation area situated on the shore of beautiful Lake Cachuma. It has over 500 campsites, many of which are shaded by oaks or other trees. Some sites have views of the lake and of the chaparral-covered hills with oaks along the ridge, across the lake. Three *yurts* are reservable—small, Siberian-style cabins.

There is enough here and nearby to keep most everyone happily occupied. Explore the Santa Ynez Valley, and see its old Spanish mission. The Danish village of Solvang offers bakeries, gift shops, and arts and crafts galleries. Also visit Santa Ynez Valley Historical Museum in the town of Santa Ynez.

The recreation area offers boating and fishing. It features a marina, bait and tackle shop, fish-cleaning tables, boat launch, and dock, all in the eastern part of the recreation area. Two piers are provided elsewhere: the larger is in the southeastern area; the other is in the southwestern area and is wheelchair accessible.

Bring your own boat or rent a motorboat, sailboat, or rowboat. A boating permit is required, and no kayaks, canoes, or boats under 10 feet in length are permitted. Inquire about other boating and sailing regulations that apply. Two-hour nature boat cruises are offered on the lake, for a fee; reservations are recommended. The lake is stocked with rainbow trout. Bass, catfish, perch, and bluegill can also be caught. Fishing requires a license.

The Nature Center, near the store, presents displays of Chumash artifacts, and of local plant and animal life, and has a gift shop. Summer nature walks are conducted. There are lake-view picnic areas (with picnic tables and barbecues), playgrounds, hiking trails, a snack bar, and a rentable recreation hall.

During summer, in the southern part of the recreation area, the miniature golf course and video arcade are open, bicycles may be rented, and swimming in the pool is permitted (fee: see below). In the northern part of the recreation area, summer astronomy programs are given at the outdoor amphitheater.

Groceries, ice, propane, gasoline, and other supplies are available all year at Cachuma Lake Store, centrally located. Supplies are available in Santa Ynez and Solvang, about 11 and 14 miles west, respectively. For more information, write Santa Barbara County Parks Department or phone the recreation area.

SITES, FEES, FACILITIES, RESTRICTIONS *Individual (or family) campsites.* All individual sites are numbered and nonreservable. For RVs, there are 90 sites with full hookups and 38 sites with partial hookups (electricity and water); the nightly fee is $21 per site ($18 for senior citizens). For tents or RVs, there are over 400 non-hookup sites; the nightly fee is $15 per site ($13 for senior citizens). Up to eight people and two vehicles are allowed at each site. The nightly fee for the second vehicle is $8. Special weekly rates are available during fall and winter; phone for details.

Each individual, full-hookup site has a picnic table only. Each of the other individual sites has a picnic table and has a steel fire ring (with grill), or a steel pedestal barbecue, or a small concrete barbecue. Some sites have both a fire ring and a barbecue. Some sites have blacktop parking spurs, and others have grass spurs.

Group sites. There are nine group sites that vary in fee according to size, and take from 8 to 30 vehicles. Phone for group camping fees. Reservations are required, for a nonrefundable fee of $25.

Each group site has picnic tables, a preparation table, a large concrete barbecue, and a rock fire ring for group campfires.

The recreation area has several restrooms with sinks and flush toilets, and some also with pay showers. Other facilities include water spigots, drinking fountains, a coin laundromat (near the entrance), dumpsters, a mailbox (at the full-hookup area), information boards, and a centrally located RV dump station. Pay phones are available near the entrance and at the restrooms.

Some restrooms and some campsites (with concrete pads) are wheelchair accessible. Hard-surface paths have been provided.

Day-use fees (per day) are $5 per vehicle, $5 per boat, and $2 per dog. The swimming pool is open from Memorial Day to Labor Day, and the fee is $1 per person, per hour.

Cachuma Lake Recreation Area is usually open. Camping limit is 14 days. Quiet hours are from 10 P.M. to 7 A.M. Youths 17 years of age or under must be accompanied by an adult. No swimming, water-skiing, or wind-surfing is permitted on the lake because it is a drinking water source. Maximum RV length is 40 feet. Fires are permitted only in the recreation area's barbecues and fire rings, or in approved containers. No plants, animals, rocks, or other natural features may be removed, as all are protected by law.

The nightly fee or day-use fee is $2 for each pet. Pets must be leashed and kept at least 50 feet away from the shoreline. No pets are permitted in boats. Owners must clean up after their pets.

DIRECTIONS From central Santa Barbara, take U.S. Highway 101 about 4 miles west to the State Highway 154 exit. Go north on Highway 154, about 18 miles, to Cachuma Lake entrance road. Turn right (north). Signs direct you around the recreation area.

Fremont Campground
U.S. Forest Service

GENERAL SETTING (LOCATION, FEATURES, SUPPLIES, INFORMATION) A pleasant river valley, surrounded by hills spotted with oaks and chaparral, is the setting for this campground. It is situated on a slightly inclined slope next to Paradise Road and is well shaded by large-limbed oaks. The campsites are separated from each other in little clearings and have some privacy. A camp host resides at Campsite 4. Fishing is permitted at the Santa Ynez River, stocked with trout in the spring season (license required).

The camp is at a good location for exploring Solvang and Santa Barbara, being nearly midway between them. For more on the Lower Santa Ynez Recreation Area, see Paradise Campground and

Upper Oso Campground in this book. Limited supplies, firewood, ice, bait, and pay phones are available at Paradise Store and Grill, on Paradise Road just east of Highway 154. From there it's a trip of roughly 15 miles on Highway 154 to Santa Barbara (southeast) or to Santa Ynez and Solvang (northwest) for supplies.

For more information, phone the concessionaire, or contact the Santa Barbara Ranger District of the Los Padres National Forest.

SITES, FEES, FACILITIES, RESTRICTIONS There are 15 non-reservable, numbered sites for tents or RVs (no hookups). Some sites have their own paved parking spurs. Other sites share small paved parking areas close to the sites. The camp road is paved. The nightly fee is $12 per site. Up to eight persons and two vehicles are allowed at each site. The nightly fee for the second vehicle is $4. The day-use fee is $5 per vehicle.

Each site has a picnic table, a pedestal barbecue, and a rock-and-metal fire ring (without grill). The camp has water spigots, pedal-flush toilets, dumpsters, and an information board.

The camp is open from May 30 to November 1. Camping limit is 14 days. Quiet time is from 10 P.M. to 6 A.M. Maximum RV length is 16 feet. Fires are permitted only in the camp's barbecues and fire rings. Dogs must be leashed.

DIRECTIONS From central Santa Barbara, take U.S. Highway 101 about 4 miles west to State Highway 154. Go north on Highway 154 about 10.5 miles to Paradise Road. Turn right, and go about 2.5 miles to camp, on the road's right (south) side.

Paradise Campground
U.S. Forest Service

GENERAL SETTING (LOCATION, FEATURES, SUPPLIES, INFORMATION) This is one of five popular camps that lie within the Lower Santa Ynez Recreation Area, east of Cachuma Lake, and west of Gibraltar Reservoir. The recreation area stretches roughly 10 miles over a small inhabited river valley that contains a number of modest ranch-style homes. This area is the exact opposite of the Upper Santa Ynez Recreation Area, east of Gibraltar Reservoir, where there is little sign of civilization. Families and camping groups tend to prefer the Lower area, with its developed campgrounds, store, forest station, and sense of community. Rugged individualists would rather have the Upper area with its wide-open spaces, primitive little camps, quietude, and few signs of life other than birds and deer. For more about the Lower Santa Ynez Recreation Area, see Upper Oso Campground in this book. Campsites are set on a partly shaded oak flat on a paved loop next to the main road. The flat sits at a level slightly below that of the main road, giving a sense of separation. The weather here is best for camping during spring and fall. Rain comes in winter, and heat in summer, although fog from the ocean brings some relief.

Santa Ynez is a common local name. The camp lies within the Lower Santa Ynez Recreation Area, in Santa Ynez Canyon, close by the Santa Ynez River that flows along the northern base of the Santa Ynez Mountains. The town of Santa Ynez and the Spanish-flavored mission are next door to the Danish-flavored town of Solvang, in the Santa Ynez Valley. Fishing is permitted at the Santa Ynez River, stocked with trout during spring (license required).

Limited supplies, firewood, ice, bait, and pay phones are available at Paradise Store and Grill, on Paradise Road just east of Highway 154. From that point, it's a trip of roughly 15 miles on Highway 154 to Santa Barbara (southeast) or to Santa Ynez and Solvang (northwest), for a wider variety of supplies.

For more information, phone the concessionaire, or contact the Santa Barbara Ranger District of the Los Padres National Forest.

SITES, FEES, FACILITIES, RESTRICTIONS There are 15 numbered sites for tents or RVs, with dirt-and-gravel spurs. The camp's loop road is paved. The nightly fee is $12 per site. Up to eight people and two vehicles are allowed at each site. The nightly fee for the second vehicle is $4. Some sites are reservable. The day-use fee is $5 per vehicle.

Each site has a picnic table, a pedestal barbecue, a rock-and-metal fire ring (without grill) or a steel fire ring (with grill). The camp has water spigots, pedal-flush toilets, dumpsters, and an information board, but no hookups. A camp host resides in camp.

This camp is usually open, but is subject to closure during rains or fires. Camping limit is 14 days. Quiet hours are from 10 P.M. to 6 A.M. Maximum RV length is 22 feet. Fires are permitted only in the camp's barbecues and fire rings. Dogs must be leashed.

DIRECTIONS From central Santa Barbara, take U.S. Highway 101 about 4 miles west to State Highway 154. Go north on Highway 154 about 10.5 miles to Paradise Road. Turn right, and go about 3 miles to camp, on the right (south) side of the road.

Los Prietos Campground
U.S. Forest Service

GENERAL SETTING (LOCATION, FEATURES, SUPPLIES, INFORMATION) This inviting camp in the Lower Santa Ynez Recreation area sits on an oak-forested slope that is not too steep. Some sites have views of the chaparral-covered coastal hills. Fishing is permitted at the Santa Ynez River, stocked with trout during spring (license required). The camp's elevation is 1000 feet. For more about the area, see Paradise Campground in this book.

White Rock Picnic Area, nicely shaded by oaks, is about a quarter mile west of camp, on the north side of Paradise Road. For picnic facilities, see below. Snyder Trail, for hiking only, is reached by taking Paradise Road a mile east of camp. This steep trail leads south, about 6 miles, up to East Camino Cielo which traverses the ridge of the Santa Ynez Mountains. For more about the Lower Santa Ynez Recreation Area, see Paradise Campground and Upper Oso Campground in this book. A camp host resides at Site 1.

At Los Prietos Ranger Station, about a mile east of camp, a pay phone and a portable toilet are provided. Limited supplies, firewood, ice, bait, and pay phones are available at Paradise Store and Grill, on Paradise Road just east of Highway 154. Supplies are also available in Santa Barbara and Solvang.

For more information, phone the concessionaire, or contact the Santa Barbara Ranger District of the Los Padres National Forest.

SITES, FEES, FACILITIES, RESTRICTIONS There are 37 non-reservable, numbered sites for tents or RVs, for $12 per site, per night. The limit is eight people and two vehicles per site. The nightly fee for the second vehicle is $4. Sites have blacktop spurs or share small parking lots. The day-use fee is $5 per vehicle.

Each campsite has a picnic table, a pedestal barbecue, and a steel fire ring with grill. The camp has water spigots, pedal-flush toilets, a dumpster, and an information board, but no hookups.

White Rock Picnic Area has 27 picnic sites, each with a picnic table and a pedestal barbecue. It has a paved parking area, dumpsters, piped water, and pedal-flush toilets with wheelchair access. A vehicle parked only for day use requires an Adventure Pass (fee).

The camp is usually open, but is subject to closure during rains or fires. Camping limit is 14 days. Quiet time is from 10 P.M. to 6 A.M. Maximum RV length is 22 feet. Fires are permitted only in the camp's barbecues and fire rings, and in the picnic area's barbecues. Dogs must be leashed.

DIRECTIONS From central Santa Barbara, take U.S. Highway 101 about 4 miles west to State Highway 154. Go north on Highway 154 about 10.5 miles to Paradise Road. Turn right, and go about 4 miles to camp, on the right (south) side of the road.

Sage Hill Group Camp
U.S. Forest Service

GENERAL SETTING (LOCATION, FEATURES, SUPPLIES, INFORMATION) The only group camp in the Lower Santa Ynez Recreation Area sits just north of the Santa Ynez River, in an open spot next to the hills. Oak trees shade portions of the camp.

The camp has five group loops: Loop 1, Sycamore; Loop 2, Live Oak; Loop 3, Pine; Loop 4, Cactus; and Loop 5, Caballo. Equestrian camping is available at Loop 5, Caballo, with features such as hitching posts, a dozen corrals, and access to miles of horseback riding trails. The Spanish word *caballo*, in fact, means *horse*.

The Santa Ynez River is stocked with trout during spring; fishing requires a license. For hikers, the steep Aliso Canyon Nature Trail is reached near the equestrian camping loop, and follows Aliso Creek about 1.5 miles to Upper Oso Campground. For more about the Lower Santa Ynez Recreation Area, see Paradise Campground and Upper Oso Campground in this book.

A pay phone is located near camp at Los Prietos Ranger Station. Limited supplies, firewood, ice, bait, and pay phones are available at Paradise Store and Grill, on Paradise Road just east of Highway 154. From that point, it's a trip of roughly 15 miles to Santa Barbara (southeast) or to Solvang (northwest) for supplies.

For more information, phone the concessionaire, or contact the Santa Barbara Ranger District of the Los Padres National Forest.

SITES, FEES, FACILITIES, RESTRICTIONS All five loops are for tents or RVs. The nightly fee, for Loops 1 through 4, is $50 per loop, with at least 25 people and up to 56 people per loop. Larger groups may reserve both Loops 3 and 4. The nightly fee for equestrian Loop 5 is $60. There is also a service charge of $8 per loop, on the first day only, and reservations are required. Loops 1, 2, and 5 have paved parking spurs for RVs. Camp roads and parking lots at Loops 3 and 4 are paved and have some wheelchair access.

Each group loop has a few picnic tables surrounding a large, steel-and-concrete fire ring. Each loop also has a service table, a large brick barbecue, a small pedestal barbecue, water spigots, and two pedal-flush toilets. Oaks shade Loops 3, 4, and 5. The camp has dumpsters and an information board, but no hookups. The camp is usually open, but is subject to closure during rains and fires. Camping limit is 14 days. Quiet hours are from 10 P.M. to 6 A.M. Maximum RV length is 30 feet. Fires are permitted only in the camp's barbecues and fire rings. Dogs must be leashed.

DIRECTIONS From central Santa Barbara, take U.S. Highway 101 about 4 miles west to State Highway 154. Go north on Highway 154 about 10.5 miles to Paradise Road. Turn right, and go about 5 miles to Forest Road 28W05, at Los Prietos Ranger Station. Turn left (north) and go about half a mile to camp.

Upper Oso Campground
U.S. Forest Service

GENERAL SETTING (LOCATION, FEATURES, SUPPLIES, INFORMATION) This camp is located in chaparral-covered Oso Canyon, in the eastern Lower Santa Ynez Recreation Area. *Oso*, a word from old Spain, means *bear*, an old woodland critter. The camp sits at a wide place in the canyon, just ahead of where the canyon becomes narrow, so the camp appears to have canyon walls on three sides. Sites are spread out, and some are shaded by oaks or sycamores. Winters are frequently rainy, and summer heat is lessened, to a degree, by coastal fog. The elevation is 1100 feet.

This camp features five equestrian sites and 14 corrals for horses, at its north end, with access to miles of equestrian trails. Santa Cruz Trail is reached at Santa Cruz Trailhead parking area. This steep trail, for hiking and horseback riding only, leads north from camp about 1.5 miles to Nineteen Oaks Camp, a little hike-in camp. Phone regarding fire permits and camp information.

Camuesa Road, for off-highway vehicle (OHV) use, begins at Upper Oso Camp and extends several miles eastward. OHV drivers must display their OHV Green Stickers. Only two-wheeled vehicles and all-terrain vehicles (ATVs) are permitted on this road.

Several picnic areas are southeast of camp. Lower Oso Picnic Area sits at the mouth of Oso Canyon, where Paradise Road meets Forest Road 5N15, the road that leads to Upper Oso Camp. At this crossroad, Paradise Road becomes Santa Ynez River Road. This road is crossed in several places by the Santa Ynez River, and is closed during rainy weather.

When Santa Ynez River Road is open, you can continue east, about 1.5 miles, to Falls Picnic Area, at the right (south) side of the road, set on an oak-shaded bank next to the river. Go half a mile farther east, through a tunnel of trees, and pass what's left of old Santa Ynez Camp, on the right, including a field of weeds, a locked gate, and a warning sign that says CAMPGROUND CLOSED. No camping, picnicking, or any other use is permitted there. Birds and squirrels are among the few residents in the old camp now.

Go about 1.25 miles farther, on Santa Ynez River Road, and pass Matias Potrero Connector Trail (27W25), for hiking only, on the right. Go a quarter mile to Live Oak Picnic Area, on the right, perched above the Santa Ynez River on an oak bluff. The bluff and river lie within a gorge. Go half a mile farther to Red Rock Picnic Area on the left, a walk-in picnic area with very limited parking. It is situated between the road and river, in a glen full of oaks and sycamores. It was once a camp, but a sign says CAMPGROUND CLOSED.

Continue half a mile farther to the end of the road and Gateway Trailhead's two parking areas, about a tenth mile apart. Two roads, open to hiking but closed to vehicles, lead east about 2 miles to Gibraltar Reservoir, where no swimming is permitted, since it is a drinking water source. The parking areas have portable chemical toilets, and the second area also has dumpsters and a trailhead information board. For picnic area facilities, see below.

Limited supplies, firewood, ice, bait, and pay phones are available at Paradise Store and Grill, on Paradise Road just east of Highway 154. Supplies are also available in Santa Barbara.

For more information, phone the concessionaire, or contact the Santa Barbara Ranger District of the Los Padres National Forest.

SITES, FEES, FACILITIES, RESTRICTIONS There are 20 nonreservable sites for tents or RVs, for $12 per site, per night. There are five reservable equestrian sites for $14 per site, per night. Each site takes up to eight people and two vehicles. The nightly fee for the second vehicle is $4. The day-use fee is $5 per vehicle. Some sites have blacktop spurs, a few of which take longer trailers or motorhomes. Other sites share small parking areas.

Each site has a picnic table, a pedestal barbecue, and a steel fire ring with grill. The camp has water spigots, pedal-flush toilets, dumpsters, and an information board, but no hookups.

Lower Oso Picnic Area has 23 picnic sites, Falls Picnic Area has 4 picnic sites, Live Oak Picnic Area has 7 picnic sites, and Red Rock Picnic Area has 28 picnic sites. At each area, each picnic site has a picnic table and a pedestal barbecue. Some sites at Red Rock have two tables each. Lower Oso has piped water and pedal-flush toilets, Falls and Live Oak each have a portable chemical toilet, and Red Rock has vault toilets and a dumpster. Lower Oso has a parking lot. Parking is very limited at the other picnic areas, especially at Red Rock. Again, the access road, Santa Ynez River Road, is closed during the rainy season. Picnic areas are open daily from 6 A.M. to 8 P.M. A vehicle parked for day use only, at a picnic area or trailhead, requires an Adventure Pass (fee).

The camp is usually open, but is subject to closure during rains or fires. Camping limit is 14 days. Quiet time is from 10 P.M. to 6 A.M. Maximum RV length is 22 feet. For fires, use only the camp's and picnic areas' barbecues and fire rings. Dogs must be leashed.

DIRECTIONS From central Santa Barbara, take U.S. Highway 101 about 4 miles west to State Highway 154. Exit, turn right (north) and go about 10.5 miles to Paradise Road. Turn right, and go about 6 miles to Forest Road 5N15 (Romero Camuesa Road, according to the sign). Turn left (north) and go 1.5 miles to camp.

Juncal Campground
U.S. Forest Service

GENERAL SETTING (LOCATION, FEATURES, SUPPLIES, INFORMATION) This primitive tent camp is located roughly 35 miles northeast of Santa Barbara, in the remote Pendola area, within the Upper Santa Ynez Recreation Area. The campground sits in a well-shaded oak flat, beside the road, near the Santa Ynez River. The elevation is 1800 feet. Juncal Road is closed to motor vehicles, but open to hiking, at the eastern edge of camp. It leads east from camp, roughly 2 miles, to Jameson Lake, then to a more remote part of the Upper Santa Ynez Recreation Area.

The road to the Pendola area, and to camp, traverses the ridge of the Santa Ynez Mountains and is a lengthy one. This road starts out as Forest Road 5N12, also called East Camino Cielo. *Camino cielo* means *sky way* in Spanish and is a fitting name for the road.

Chumash Painted Cave State Historic Park is a natural depression formed by coastal winds. Its colorful Native American paintings can be seen through a grate that protects them. Tours are offered, but this state park has no facilities or wheelchair access. From Highway 154, take East Camino Cielo east about 2 miles to Painted Cave Road. Turn right (south) and go about 2 miles up a steep, winding road to an area of limited parking, then walk about 75 feet farther.

Continuing along East Camino Cielo, when visibility is good, stop and get out to enjoy the impressive view of the Pacific Ocean and Channel Islands to the south. The rugged Santa Ynez River Valley, to the north, can also be seen during the drive.

Cold Spring Trail (26W10) reaches East Camino Cielo about 14 miles east of Highway 154, at Cold Spring Saddle. A trailhead parking area is provided on the south side of the road. The northbound trail is reached west of the trailhead parking area. It leads north about 2 miles to Forbush Flat, then about 3 miles farther to Mono Camp, beyond the Santa Ynez River. Phone for information on trail camps in Forbush and Blue canyons. The southbound trail heads south from the parking area, in the direction of the ocean, about 4 miles to Mountain Drive in Montecito. Just east of the trailhead parking area, another little trail winds its way up the ridge above the road, and offers great views of the ocean and islands to the south. No motor vehicles are allowed on these trails.

Divide Peak Road is designated for off-highway vehicle (OHV) use only. It is reached by continuing east on East Camino Cielo from Cold Spring Trail, for about 4 miles. Near the point where the pavement ends, a crossroad is reached; a short road leads to the left (north) and to the parking area; Divide Peak Road leads to the right (south). Divide Peak Road wanders south and east through the hills, for over 10 miles, to Divide Peak. Only motorcycles and all-terrain vehicles (ATVs) are allowed to use Divide Peak Road, and on each of these vehicles an OHV Green Sticker must be displayed.

Continuing on the main road, Trail 26W12 is reached about 2.5 miles east of Divide Peak Road. This steep trail leads northwest toward Blue Canyon. Horseback riding is permitted on Trail 26W12, but no vehicles are allowed.

Purchase supplies and gasoline in Santa Barbara before the long drive to camp. For more information write or phone the Santa Barbara Ranger District of the Los Padres National Forest.

SITES, FEES, FACILITIES, RESTRICTIONS There are nine dirt sites for tents (no developed spurs), with up to eight people at each site. A parked vehicle requires an Adventure Pass (fee).

Each site has a picnic table and a steel fire ring with grill. Each of seven sites also has a pedestal barbecue. The camp has two vault toilets, but no water. An information board is at the entrance. Pay phones are located next door to San Marcos Ranger Station, just east of Highway 154, roughly 23 miles west of camp. *Note:* this camp has been temporarily closed for the protection of endangered species. It is usually open otherwise, but is subject to closure during rains. *Caution:* the camp is accessed by dirt roads, portions of which are bumpy and crossed by streams. Four-wheel-drive vehicles are recommended, but not trailers or motorhomes. Road signs warn of fire danger, flooding, and substandard road conditions after storms. Camping limit is 14 days.

No sites are reservable. Fires are permitted only in the camp's barbecues and fire rings. Dogs must be leashed.

DIRECTIONS From central Santa Barbara, take U.S. Highway 101 about 4 miles west to the State Highway 154 exit. Exit and go north on Highway 154 about 8 miles to East Camino Cielo (Forest Road 5N12). Turn right (east), passing San Marcos Ranger Station and pay phones. Continue east, for about 19 miles, to a crossroad and a sign that says END OF HIGHWAY VEHICLE ROUTE—RECREATION AREA AHEAD. (The dirt road to the right is Divide Peak Road, for OHV use only, and becomes Forest Road 5N12.) Continue straight ahead (east) on Forest Road 5N15, over a bumpy, dirt stretch, for about 4 miles. Just east of a river crossing, the camp sits at a crossroad (camp sign missing). Leaving Forest Road 5N15, go east on Juncal Road, through the camp entrance.

Middle Santa Ynez Campground
P-Bar Flats Campground
U.S. Forest Service

GENERAL SETTING (LOCATION, FEATURES, SUPPLIES, INFORMATION) These two Pendola area camps, within the Upper Santa Ynez Recreation Area, are located roughly 40 miles northeast of Santa Barbara. The Pendola area is rural and very remote; other than a few campgrounds and debris dams, there are hardly any other signs of civilization. The old Pendola Forest Station, closed as of this writing, was just east of Middle Santa Ynez Camp, on Big Caliente Road. Trails for hiking, horseback riding, bicycling, and motorcycling are the basis of Pendola's popularity.

These primitive tent camps are a mile apart and close to the Santa Ynez River, where fishing is permitted (license required). The elevation at Middle Santa Ynez Camp is 1500 feet, and at P-Bar Flats Camp, 1800 feet. Each camp is set on an oak flat next to the road. Sites are set along a camp loop road inside each camp.

Middle Santa Ynez Campground is the larger of the two camps and is adjacent to the river. Its sites are well spread out over a quarter mile of flat land in the bottom of the canyon, and are comfortably shaded by tall oaks. *Middle* was originally included in the camp's name to distinguish it from two other camps: the closed Santa Ynez Camp, west of Gibraltar Reservoir, and Upper Santa Ynez Camp, a hike-in camp, east of Jameson Lake.

P-Bar Flats Campground is set on a small oak flat, next to a hill. This little camp sits across the road from the Santa Ynez River, and affords a pleasant view of an oak grove to the east. Large oaks with thick, spread-out limbs afford shade at campsites. Local signs show the camp's name as *P-Bar*, but Forest Service maps and tabulations include *Flats* or *Flat*.

Big Caliente Road (Forest Road 5N16), just east of Middle Santa Ynez Camp, leads about 2 miles north to Lower Caliente Picnic Area (not to be confused with Little Caliente near Mono Camp). About a mile north of Lower Caliente is Big Caliente Hot Springs. Lower Caliente Picnic Area has two picnic sites (per U.S. Forest Service). Big Caliente Road was closed for repairs, as of this writing, so picnic area information was not verifiable on site.

Blue Canyon Trail is reached about a mile west of P-Bar Flats Camp, and leads south to Blue Canyon. Phone for information on trail camps in Blue and Forbush Canyons. For information on other hiking trails and motorcycle trails, on the way to Middle Santa Ynez and P-Bar Flats Camps, and for information on Chumash Painted Cave State Park, see Juncal Campground in this book.

Purchase supplies and gasoline in Santa Barbara before making the long trip to the camps. For more information, contact the Santa Barbara Ranger District of the Los Padres National Forest.

SITES, FEES, FACILITIES, RESTRICTIONS Middle Santa Ynez Camp has nine tent sites. P-Bar Flats Camp has four tent sites. Each site takes up to eight people. Each camp has a dirt loop road (no RV spurs). A parked vehicle requires an Adventure Pass.

At both camps, each site has a picnic table, a pedestal barbecue, and a steel fire ring with grill. Two sites at Middle Santa

Ynez Camp have two tables each. Middle Santa Ynez Camp has three vault toilets, and P-Bar Flats Camp has two vault toilets. Middle Santa Ynez Camp has two information boards, and P-Bar Flats Camp has one. The camps have no water. Pay phones are located next door to San Marcos Ranger Station, just east of Highway 154, roughly 27 miles southwest of the camps.

The camps and roads are usually open, but are subject to closure during rains. *Caution:* portions of the roads are made of clay and dirt, are rutty, and are slippery and impassable during rains. Four-wheel-drive vehicles are recommended, but not trailers or motorhomes. Road signs warn of possible fire danger, flooding, and substandard road conditions after storms.

Camping limit is 14 days. No sites at either camp are reservable. Quiet time is from 10 P.M. to 6 A.M. Fires are permitted only in the camps' barbecues and fire rings. Dogs must be leashed.

DIRECTIONS Use directions for Juncal Campground, but at the crossroad where Juncal Camp sits, bear to the left (north) on Forest Road 5N15 (Camuesa Road). Go about 3 miles to Middle Santa Ynez Camp, on the left (south) side of the road (camp sign missing). Go about a mile farther to P-Bar Flats Camp, on the right.

Mono Campground
U.S. Forest Service

GENERAL SETTING (LOCATION, FEATURES, SUPPLIES, INFORMATION) This is the most remote of the Upper Santa Ynez Recreation Area's road camps. It sits at the end of the line, being not far from a locked gate, beyond which the main road is closed to motor vehicles. This small, primitive tent camp lies east of Gibraltar Reservoir, near Mono Creek, in a wetland meadow.

The camp's remoteness should please rugged outdoor individuals who crave solitude. The camp has one drive-in campsite and three walk-in campsites. The elevation is 1500 feet. Shade is provided, hours before sunset, by a stone hill across the creek, to the west. Earlier in the day, oaks and sycamores provide the shade.

The drive-in campsite is situated close to the main road, near the entrance, and is out in the open. Just north of this site is the trailhead of the trail that leads about 500 feet northwest to the three walk-in sites. Those sites are situated in an oak-shaded glen near Mono Creek. From there, Mono Debris Dam is about 500 feet farther northwest via the trail through the narrow canyon. On the trail, hiking, horseback riding, and bicycling are permitted, but not motor vehicles.

Continue on Camuesa Road about half a mile beyond Mono Camp and reach Little Caliente Trail. It leads to the right (northeast) toward Little Caliente Hot Springs, a day-use-only area. On Camuesa Road, north of this trail, you reach the locked Mono Gate. From there the road continues northwest, but is restricted to hiking, horseback riding, and bicycling; no motor vehicles are allowed.

About half a mile before reaching camp, a hiking trail leads west about a quarter mile to the Mono Adobe, then another quarter mile to Gibraltar Reservoir. After about another half mile, Cold Spring Trail is reached. It wanders south about 4 miles and reaches the trailhead parking area on East Camino Cielo, about 14 miles east of Highway 154. The trail is steep in places.

For information about other trails, on the way to Mono Camp, see Juncal and Middle Santa Ynez Campgrounds in this book. Signs in the vicinity remind visitors that this is a protected wildlife area.

Purchase supplies and gasoline in Santa Barbara before making the long trip to this camp. For more information, contact the Santa Barbara Ranger District of the Los Padres National Forest.

SITES, FEES, FACILITIES, RESTRICTIONS There are four nonreservable dirt sites for tents. Up to eight people are allowed at each site. A parked vehicle requires an Adventure Pass (fee).

Each campsite has a picnic table and a steel fire ring with grill. The camp has two vault toilets, close to the walk-in sites, but has no water. An information board is provided near the entrance. Pay phones are located next door to San Marcos Ranger Station, just east of Highway 154, roughly 31 miles southwest of camp.

The camp and access roads are usually open, but are subject to closure during rains. *Caution:* the lengthy, poor, clay-and-dirt roads are crossed by streams and are slippery and impassable in wet weather. Four-wheel-drive vehicles are recommended, but not trailers or motorhomes. Road signs alert you to possibilities of fire danger, flooding, and substandard road conditions after storms.

Camping limit is 14 days. No fires are permitted except in the camp's fire rings. Dogs must be leashed.

DIRECTIONS Use directions for Juncal Camp, but at the crossroad where Juncal Camp sits, bear to the left (north) on Forest Road 5N15 (Camuesa Road). Go about 7.7 miles to camp (camp sign missing, as of this writing).

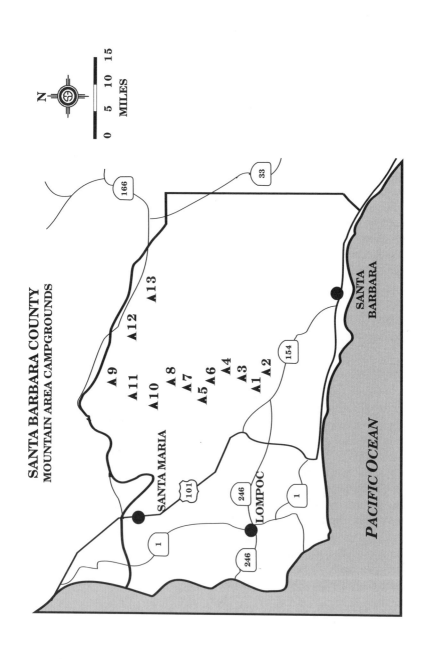

SANTA BARBARA COUNTY
MOUNTAIN AREA CAMPGROUNDS

SANTA BARBARA COUNTY
MOUNTAIN AREA

Davy Brown Campground

Figueroa Campground
U.S. Forest Service

GENERAL SETTING (LOCATION, FEATURES, SUPPLIES, IN-FORMATION) The Figueroa Mountain Recreation Area, northeast of Solvang, is the location of this well-liked, hillside campground, with sites set in a forest of pines and other native trees. The elevation is over 3500 feet at camp, and is over 4500 feet at nearby Figueroa Mountain summit. Near camp, the Santa Ynez Valley can be seen, in the distance to the southwest, from the main road. Enjoy the drive up Figueroa Mountain from Los Olivos to the campground. The road wanders through little oak-dotted valleys with cattle grazing, then along the mountain with terrific views. Wildflowers add to the area's beauty during spring.

Solvang's quaint village is a taste of old Denmark, and the stately mission, near there, is a taste of old Spain. Solvang and the mission are located in the nearby Santa Ynez Valley and are worth visiting during your stay in the Figueroa Mountain area.

La Jolla Trail (30W10) is reached about a mile west of camp on the north side of Figueroa Mountain Road. A 5-mile hike down this steep trail takes you to the bottom of Birabent Canyon and to tiny Ballard Camp near La Jolla Spring. Spring water must be purified before drinking. No motor vehicles are allowed on the trail. Phone for trail camp and fire permit information.

Figueroa Mountain has several small picnic areas, including one on the summit with a wonderful view. About half a mile west of camp, turn north on unpaved, winding Forest Road 8N16, and go about 1.5 miles to a fork. If you bear to the left (south) you enter Pino Alto Picnic Area on an unpaved loop road. *Pino alto*, in Spanish, means *high pine* or *tall pine*. Either way, this is an apt description, since the pines here are at a high elevation (4400 feet) and are tall. Pino Alto Nature Trail is a half-mile paved path that wanders from the picnic area through the pine forest and is wheelchair accessible. An information board is provided. The picnic area has four picnic sites, each with a picnic table and a pedestal barbecue. One picnic site and the vault toilet have wheelchair access.

Back at the fork, near Pino Alto Picnic Area, bear to the north and continue on Forest Road 8N16. Go about a quarter mile to the short turnoff that leads to Figueroa Vista Point and Figueroa Lookout Picnic Area. Both are just beyond the fire lookout tower on the summit of Figueroa Mountain. At 4500 feet, the summit commands a thrilling, 270-degree view of the rugged San Rafael Wilderness to the north and east, and of the mountainous territory to the west. *Caution:* don't go near the edge because there is a steep drop-off and no fence. An information plaque is provided. The picnic area has two picnic tables and two vault toilets (no barbecues). Scattered pines on the summit add atmosphere.

Return to Forest Road 8N16 and go west about a quarter mile to Cumbre Picnic Area on a loop at the end of the road. Appropriately, the Spanish word *cumbre* means *summit*. The picnic area is nestled in a beautiful pine forest, at an elevation of 4200 feet. It has a picnic table, a pedestal barbecue, and a vault toilet. Take Forest Road 8N16 back down to Figueroa Mountain Road (Forest Road 7N07). Turn west and go about half a mile to Catway Road (Forest Road 8N01), an OHV road designated for four-wheel-drive vehicles and motorcycles only. It is a narrow, bumpy dirt road. A quarter mile north on this road is Catway Picnic Area with a picnic table and a great view from an elevation of 3600 feet.

Figueroa Forest Station is about 1.5 miles west of camp. Supplies and gasoline are available in Solvang and Buellton.

For more information, write or phone the Santa Lucia Ranger District of the Los Padres National Forest.

SITES, FEES, FACILITIES, RESTRICTIONS There are 32 numbered, nonreservable sites for tents or self-contained RVs (no hookups). A parked vehicle requires an Adventure Pass (fee). Sites have blacktop spurs, and some sites have wheelchair access.

Each site has a picnic table, a pedestal barbecue, and a steel fire ring with grill. Piped water spigots are available throughout the campground. The camp has vault toilets at three locations. At Figueroa Fire Station, about 1.5 miles west, a pay phone is available, and two trash dumpsters are provided during summer.

The camp is usually open, but it and local picnic areas, roads, and trails are subject to closure during rains, snows, and fires. Camping limit is 14 days. Quiet hours are from 10 P.M. to 6 A.M. Maximum RV length is 22 feet. Fires are permitted from May 1 to November 15; use only the camp's and picnic areas' barbecues and fire rings. Carry out your trash. Dogs must leashed.

DIRECTIONS From U.S. Highway 101, about 5.5 miles north of Buellton, take State Highway 154 east about 3 miles to Figueroa Mountain Road (Forest Road 7N07) in Los Olivos, in the Santa Ynez Valley. Turn left (north) and go about 13 miles to camp.

Cachuma Campground
U.S. Forest Service

GENERAL SETTING (LOCATION, FEATURES, SUPPLIES, INFORMATION) Not to be confused with Cachuma Lake Recreation Area, this small, primitive campground is not at Lake Cachuma, but is more than 5 miles north of there, in the Figueroa Mountain Recreation Area. The elevation is 2200 feet.

The camp is on the east side of Happy Canyon Road. Parallel to this road is a narrow dirt road, along which the sites are spread out in a partly shaded glen of sycamores. A creek runs along the east side of camp, and the fresh mountain air is permeated with the spicy fragrance of sagebrush. Volcanic peaks and formations can be observed in the Happy Canyon area, on the way to camp.

A Spanish mission and a Danish village (Solvang) are located in the Santa Ynez Valley about 15 miles southwest of camp. Santa Ynez Valley Historical Museum exhibits Chumash artifacts.

Supplies and gasoline are available in Solvang and Buellton. For more information, write or phone the Santa Lucia Ranger District of the Los Padres National Forest.

SITES, FEES, FACILITIES, RESTRICTIONS The camp has six nonreservable dirt sites for tents or self-contained RVs (no hookups). A parked vehicle requires an Adventure Pass (fee).

Each site has a picnic table and a chopping block resembling a tree stump. Two sites each have a steel fire ring (with grill), and three sites each have a pedestal barbecue. The camp has two vault toilets, but no water or trash receptacles; carry out your trash.

The camp is usually open, but is subject to closure during rains and fires. *Caution:* Happy Canyon Road is mostly paved but has some potholes and a 3-mile dirt stretch near camp. It is crossed by streams in several places and is closed during landslides due to rains. Trailers and motorhomes are not recommended.

Camping limit is 14 days. Maximum RV length is 16 feet. Fires are permitted from May 1 to November 15 in the camp's barbecues and fire rings only. Dogs must be leashed.

DIRECTIONS From U.S. Highway 101 in Buellton, take State Highway 246 east about 10 miles. Just after the road bends south, turn left (east) at Happy Canyon Road. Go about 11 miles to camp, during which the road bends northeast. The camp is on the right (east) side of the road (camp sign missing, as of this writing).

The 7-mile stretch of Figueroa Mountain Road, east of Figueroa Campground, is not always open to Cachuma Saddle Station and Happy Canyon Road. When open, it offers another route to Cachuma Campground, with fine views. Caution: this road is narrow, winding, and paved, with some potholes.

Davy Brown Campground
U.S. Forest Service

GENERAL SETTING (LOCATION, FEATURES, SUPPLIES, INFORMATION) This rustic campground is located in a narrow, shaded canyon in the Sunset Valley, within the Figueroa Mountain Recreation Area, just south of the San Rafael Wilderness. Pines, firs, and chaparral grow in abundance, and golden poppies and blue lupines give the area a rich burst of color in spring. The elevation at camp is 2100 feet. Old charred skeletons of trees, on the hills in this region, are a reminder of fire danger.

Davy Brown Creek, which flows by camp, is stocked annually with trout, and fishing is available from March to May (license required). The steep Davy Brown Trail (29W03) leads from Davy Brown Camp up to Figueroa Mountain Road, to the south. Ruins of an old cabin, from mining days, can be seen by the trail. On one sign, along the road, the camp's name is spelled *Davey Brown*.

Trailheads of other trails can be found along Sunset Valley Road, on the way to camp. Sunset Valley Trail (29W04) has its trailhead about 2.3 miles southeast of camp, and White Rock Trail (29W05) has its trailhead about 3.3 miles southeast of camp.

Supplies and gasoline are available in Solvang and Buellton. For more information, write or phone the Santa Lucia Ranger District of the Los Padres National Forest.

SITES, FEES, FACILITIES, RESTRICTIONS The camp has 13 nonreservable, numbered dirt sites for tents or self-contained RVs (no hookups). A parked vehicle requires an Adventure Pass (fee).

Each site has a picnic table, a pedestal barbecue, and a steel fire ring with grill. Vault toilets are near the entrance and at the rear. There is limited water; as a precaution, bring your own. Water from the nearby spring must be purified before drinking.

Caution: this camp is usually open, but it and stream-crossed Sunset Valley Road sit in a canyon bottom that floods during rains, causing their closure. Happy Canyon Road is not recommended for trailers and motorhomes (see Cachuma Campground).

Camping limit is 14 days. Maximum RV length is 22 feet. Fires are permitted from May 1 to November 15 in the camp's barbecues and fire rings only. Carry out your trash. Dogs must be leashed.

DIRECTIONS From U.S. Highway 101 in Buellton, take State Highway 246 east about 10 miles, and just after the road bends south, turn left (east) at Happy Canyon Road. Go about 13 miles, during which the road bends northeast. At Cachuma Saddle Forest Station, go straight ahead, north (not left), and the road becomes Sunset Valley Road. Go about 3.7 miles to camp, on the left.

Figueroa Mountain Road also connects with Sunset Valley Road, but is not always open that far.

Nira Campground
U.S. Forest Service

GENERAL SETTING (LOCATION, FEATURES, SUPPLIES, INFORMATION) This oak-shaded tent camp is located in the fairly uninhabited Sunset Valley, where Sunset Valley Road ends, within the Figueroa Mountain Recreation Area. Camp elevation is 1000 feet. Nearby Manzana Creek is stocked annually with trout, and fishing is available from March to May (license required).

Nira Campground sits just south of the San Rafael Wilderness. This immense area of over 200,000 acres contains more than 20 wilderness hike-in camps, on trails, for the seasoned backpacker. Wilderness camping is beyond the scope of this book, so phone for information and for special wilderness camping regulations.

Upper Manzana Creek Trail (30W13) leads southeast into the San Rafael Wilderness, and the trailhead is found at the eastern end of Nira Campground. At the trailhead, an information board shows a map of San Rafael Wilderness. A registration notebook is provided on a pedestal to enable the U.S. Forest Service to monitor your stay, while in the wilderness, for your safety. The trail reaches southeast, along Manzana Creek, about 13 miles to the South Fork of the Sisquoc River and to the Sisquoc River Trail.

Lower Manzana Creek Trail (30W13) leads northwest into the San Rafael Wilderness, and the trailhead can be found about half a mile west of Nira Campground, on the west side of Sunset Valley Road. An information board and map, and a registration notebook are also provided there, near a spacious parking area (an Adventure Pass is required for a parked vehicle). The trail stretches northwest along Manzana Creek, and meets Lower Sisquoc River Trail where Manzana Creek meets the Sisquoc River.

Supplies and gasoline are available in Solvang and Buellton. For more information, write or phone the Santa Lucia Ranger District of the Los Padres National Forest.

SITES, FEES, FACILITIES, RESTRICTIONS Twelve nonreservable dirt sites for tents (no developed spurs) take up to eight people per site. A parked vehicle requires an Adventure Pass (fee).

Each campsite has a picnic table, a pedestal barbecue, and a steel fire ring with grill. Two vault toilets and a small parking area with wheelchair access are provided at the camp entrance. Nira Camp has no piped water. Davy Brown Camp has limited water, but as a precaution, bring your own. Carry out your trash.

Caution: the camp is usually open, but is subject to closure during rains. It and stream-crossed Sunset Valley Road are in a canyon bottom that floods easily. Happy Canyon Road is not recommended for trailers or motorhomes (see Cachuma Campground).

Camping limit is 14 days. Fires are permitted from May 1 to November 15 in the camp's barbecues and fire rings only. Dogs must be leashed.

DIRECTIONS From U.S. Highway 101 in Buellton, take State Highway 246 east about 10 miles, and just after the road bends south, turn left (east) at Happy Canyon Road. Go about 13 miles, during which the road bends northeast. At Cachuma Saddle Forest Station, go straight ahead, north (not left), and the road becomes Sunset Valley Road. Go about 5 miles, and pass Lower Manzana trailhead parking area on the left (west) side of the road. Go half a mile farther to the end of the road and Nira Campground.

Figueroa Mountain Road also connects with Sunset Valley Road, but is not always open that far.

Colson Canyon Campground
U.S. Forest Service

GENERAL SETTING (LOCATION, FEATURES, SUPPLIES, INFORMATION) This little camp is located in Colson Canyon, roughly 20 miles east of Santa Maria and 10 miles south of the Cuyama River. It is situated in an oak grove on the side of a low hill, at an elevation of 2080 feet. Narrow, oak-shrouded Buckhorn and Tepusquet canyons present picturesque scenes along the way, with a few cozy homes. The camp is also called *Colson*, but the Forest Service's brochures and website include the word *Canyon*.

Local sights to see, in Santa Maria, include an exhibit of historical aircraft at Santa Maria Museum of Flight, and general historical artifacts at Santa Maria Valley Historical Society Museum. Santa Maria has supplies. For more information, contact the Santa Lucia Ranger District of the Los Padres National Forest.

SITES, FEES, FACILITIES, RESTRICTIONS There are five nonreservable dirt sites for tents, two of which are suitable for RVs. An Adventure Pass (fee) is required for a parked vehicle.

Each site has a picnic table and a steel fire ring with grill. One tent site also has a pedestal barbecue. A primitive pit toilet (no door or roof) sits farther up the hill. The camp has no water or hookups; RVs must be self-contained. Carry out your trash.

The camp and roads are usually open, but are subject to closure during rains or fires. *Caution:* four-wheel-drive vehicles are advised, but not trailers or motorhomes, on Colson Canyon Road. It is winding, dirt, and crossed by streams. Road signs warn of fire danger, flooding, and substandard road conditions after storms.

Camping limit is 14 days. Maximum RV length is 22 feet. Fires are permitted from May 1 to November 15 in the camp's barbecue and fire rings only. Dogs must be leashed.

DIRECTIONS From U.S. Highway 101 in Santa Maria, take Betteravia Road east. After about 2.5 miles, the road becomes Foxen Canyon Road. Continue about 4.5 miles to Santa Maria Mesa Road, and turn left (heading southeast). Go about 4.5 miles to Tepusquet Road. Turn left (north) and go about 4.5 miles to unpaved Colson Canyon Road. Turn right (east) and go about 4.2 miles. Turn left at the short dirt road leading to camp.

Barrel Springs, Wagon Flat, and Lazy Campgrounds
U.S. Forest Service

GENERAL SETTING (LOCATION, FEATURES, INFORMA-TION, SUPPLIES) These small, primitive campgrounds are located east of Santa Maria and south of the Cuyama River. The names Barrel Springs and Wagon Flat are reminders of pioneer times, when horse-drawn wagons and wooden barrels were among the usual conveniences. This remote area has changed little since those days. Lazy Campground is a good name for a camp, since relaxation is a reason for camping in the first place. The elevation is 1000 feet at Barrel Springs Campground, and is 1400 feet at Wagon Flat and Lazy Campgrounds.

Kerry Canyon Trail (30W02) is an ORV trail of about 9 miles in length. It leads northeast from Lazy Camp, for about 6 miles through Kerry Canyon, to Miranda Pine Road. About 0.2 mile east, it continues north for about 3 miles to Indian Trail (31W02). No motor vehicles are allowed on Indian Trail.

While in Santa Maria, see historic aircraft at Santa Maria Flight Museum. Visit Santa Maria Historical Society Museum with its collection of artifacts from periods of local history. Supplies are available in Santa Maria. For more information, contact the Santa Lucia Ranger District of the Los Padres National Forest.

SITES, FEES, FACILITIES, RESTRICTIONS Barrel Springs Camp has six sites for tents. Wagon Flat Camp has three sites for tents or RVs (no hookups). Lazy Camp has two sites for tents. A parked vehicle requires an Adventure Pass (fee). All sites are non-reservable. The camp has dirt sites.

The camps' facilities include picnic tables, fire rings (with grills), and vault toilets, but no water. Carry out your trash.

Note: the camps and local access roads were temporarily closed for repairs, due to storm damage, at the time of this writing, so facility information was not verifiable on site. The camps and roads are usually open otherwise, but are subject to closure during rains or fires. *Caution:* the roads are winding, bumpy, dirt, crossed by streams, and are recommended for four-wheel-drive vehicles, but not for trailers or motorhomes. Road signs warn of fire danger, flooding, and substandard road conditions after storms.

Camping limit is 14 days. Maximum RV length at Wagon Flat Camp is 16 feet. Fires are allowed from May 1 to November 15 in the camps' fire rings only. Dogs must be leashed.

DIRECTIONS Use directions for Colson Canyon Camp, but stay on Colson Canyon Road and go about 4 more miles, on a winding, bumpy stretch of road, to unpaved La Brea Canyon Road. Either go straight ahead, reaching Barrel Springs Camp at about 2 miles, or turn left (north) at La Brea Canyon Road and go about 5 miles to Wagon Flat Camp. Just beyond Wagon Flat Camp, turn right (east) at unpaved Forest Road 30W29, and go a mile to Lazy Camp.

Miranda Pines Campground
U.S. Forest Service

GENERAL SETTING (LOCATION, FEATURES, SUPPLIES, INFORMATION) Enjoy the impressive, nearly 270-degree view from this tiny tent camp up near the top of Miranda Pine Mountain, at an elevation of over 4000 feet, just where the pines begin. The view alone is worth a stay here, for camping or picnicking, on the way to other destinations in this part of the forest. Miranda Pine Mountain is roughly 35 miles east of Santa Maria and is nearly halfway between that city and New Cuyama. The Cuyama River is about 10 miles north of camp. The camp is also called *Miranda Pine*, as is the mountain, but *Miranda Pines* is the name shown on Forest Service brochures and local signs.

Oak forests fill the hillsides along Sierra Madre Road, on the way up to camp, with great views of the Cuyama River Valley. Campsites are partially shaded by pines and oaks. A hiking trail leads north from camp, about a quarter mile up the top of the mountain. Timber Peak, with its pointed, angular shape, can be seen from camp, in the distance a few miles to the south (elevation: 4758 feet). Sierra Madre Road passes by there on its way southeast to McPherson Peak. From the crossroads near camp, the trip to McPherson Peak is roughly 21 miles in length.

Supplies and gasoline are available in Santa Maria and New Cuyama (limited). For more information, write or phone the Santa Lucia Ranger District of the Los Padres National Forest.

SITES, FEES, FACILITIES, RESTRICTIONS The camp has three nonreservable dirt sites for tents (no developed spurs). An Adventure Pass (fee) is required for a parked vehicle.

Each site has a picnic table and a steel fire ring with grill. A primitive pit toilet, with no door or roof, sits at the hill's edge. The camp has no piped water, so bring your own. Carry out your trash.

The camp and roads are usually open, but are subject to closure during rains or fires. *Caution:* Sierra Madre Road is a narrow, winding dirt road, of about 9 miles in length, recommended for four-wheel-drive vehicles but not trailers or motorhomes.

Camping limit is 14 days. Fires are permitted from May 1 to November 15 in the camp's fire rings only. Dogs must be leashed.

DIRECTIONS From central Santa Maria, take U.S. Highway 101 north about 3 miles to State Highway 166. Go east about 25.5

miles to unpaved Sierra Madre Road (Forest Road 32S13). Turn right (south) and go about 9 miles to Miranda Pine Road. Turn left, and go less than half a mile to the camp at the road's end.

Horseshoe Springs Campground
Brookshire Springs Campground
U.S. Forest Service

GENERAL SETTING (LOCATION, FEATURES, SUPPLIES, INFORMATION) These tiny, primitive tent camps are located roughly halfway between Santa Maria and New Cuyama. The camps were placed near each other in remote, shallow, oak-filled canyons, at elevations of about 1500 feet. They share the same area's features, so they have been included together in this book.

Both camps were named for local springs. Some Forest Service signs and maps include the words *Springs* or *Spring*, while brochures and other signs do not. The sign at Horseshoe Springs Camp was missing, as of this writing, but the sign on the ORV trail, just east of camp, says *Horseshoe Spring Spur*. The sign at Brookshire Springs Camp says *Brookshire*, but the sign pointing toward camp, two miles south, says *Brookshire Springs*.

Horseshoe Springs Campground is set in a small clearing with a few oaks that provide shade. Many oaks border the camp. A foot-high rock wall, with steps, frames the entrance, adding a home-like touch to the woodland scene. Just east of camp, Horseshoe Spring Spur, for limited ORV use, leads about a mile south up to another ORV trail (32W01) which goes along Buckhorn Ridge.

Brookshire Springs Campground has just two sites, placed apart from each other. One is near the center of camp; the other is to the south, down by Pine Canyon Creek. A cactus patch and yucca garden can be seen, at the north side of camp, near the trailhead. Indian Trail (31W02) goes northeast from Brookshire Springs Camp through Pine Canyon, for several miles, to Kerry Canyon Trail. No motor vehicles are allowed on Indian Trail.

Kerry Canyon Trail (30W02) is for limited ORV use; phone for details. It crosses Miranda Pine Road, about 3 miles west of Sierra Madre Road, between Miranda Pines Camp and Horseshoe Springs Camp. The trailhead for the northbound trail is about 0.2 mile east of the trailhead for the southbound trail. The northbound trail leads north about 3 miles to Indian Trail (31W02) which is not for motor vehicles. The southbound trail leads through Kerry

Canyon, for about 6 miles, to Lazy Camp, but the ORV portion ends at the 5-mile point. (Street-legal vehicles can reach Lazy Camp by forest roads; see Lazy Campground, in this book.)

Santa Maria has supplies. For more information, contact the Santa Lucia Ranger District of the Los Padres National Forest.

SITES, FEES, FACILITIES, RESTRICTIONS Both camps have nonreservable dirt sites for tents (no developed spurs). Horseshoe Springs has three sites, and Brookshire Springs has two sites. A parked vehicle requires an Adventure Pass. Carry out your trash.

At both camps, each site has a picnic table and a steel fire ring with grill. Each camp has two vault toilets, but no piped water. Water from springs or creeks must be purified before drinking.

The camps and roads are usually open, but are subject to closure during rains or fires. *Caution:* the narrow, winding dirt roads are not suitable for trailers or motorhomes, and four-wheel-drive vehicles are recommended. Each camp is located along a creek at the bottom of a canyon, and the road to Brookshire Springs Camp is crossed by streams, so flooding occurs easily during rains.

Camping limit is 14 days. Fires are permitted from May 1 to November 15 in the camps' fire rings only. Dogs must be leashed.

DIRECTIONS From central Santa Maria, take U.S. Highway 101 north about 3 miles to State Highway 166. Go east about 25.5 miles to unpaved Sierra Madre Road (Forest Road 32S13). Turn right (south) and go about 9 miles to Miranda Pine Road (Forest Road 11N03). Turn right (heading southwest). Go about 9.5 miles to a three-way crossroads; the sign was missing, as of this writing. Bear to the right (heading northwest) on Forest Road 11N04. Go about 2.7 miles to Horseshoe Springs Camp, on the left (south) side of the road (camp sign missing). Continue on Forest Road 11N04, about half a mile, and reach unpaved Forest Road 11N04A. Turn right (north) and go about 2 miles to Brookshire Springs Camp at the end of that road (camp sign says *Brookshire*).

Bates Canyon Campground
U.S. Forest Service

GENERAL SETTING (LOCATION, FEATURES, SUPPLIES, INFORMATION) As its name indicates, this primitive little camp is located in Bates Canyon, southwest of New Cuyama. The region's scenery is typical of Southern California's coastal valleys:

golden foothills spotted with oaks. This camp sits in an open clearing, with just a few shade trees. A manzanita thicket and oaks surround the clearing. The camp's elevation is 2900 feet. The chaparral-covered Sierra Madre Mountains can be seen from camp and are about six miles south. The ridge of these mountains is traversed by unpaved Sierra Madre Road (see Directions below).

Gasoline and supplies are available in New Cuyama (limited), in Taft and Maricopa, about 45 miles east, and in Santa Maria, about 45 miles west. For more information, contact the Santa Lucia Ranger District of the Los Padres National Forest.

SITES, FEES, FACILITIES, RESTRICTIONS Six nonreservable dirt sites are for tents or RVs (no hookups). A parked vehicle requires an Adventure Pass. Each site has a picnic table and a steel fire ring with grill. There are two vault toilets but no water.

The camp and road are usually open, but are subject to closure during rains or fires. *Caution:* portions of Bates Canyon Road are unpaved (dirt) or are poorly paved and rough, with lots of potholes. Trailers and motorhomes are not recommended.

Camping limit is 14 days. Maximum RV length is 16 feet. For fires, use only the camp's fire rings. Dogs must be leashed.

DIRECTIONS From the intersection of State Highways 166 and 33, southwest of Maricopa, take State Highway 166 west. Go about 10.5 miles, and New Cuyama is reached (a supply point). Then continue on Highway 166 about 12.5 miles to Cottonwood Canyon Road (Forest Road 11N01). Turn left (south) and go about 4.5 miles to Foothill Road. Turn right (west) and go half a mile. At the fork, continue straight ahead (not to the right) on Bates Canyon Road. Go about 2 miles, during which the road bends to the south. At the next fork, bear to the *left* (southeast) to enter the camp.

If, at this final fork, you had gone to the right (south), you would have continued on unpaved Bates Canyon Road, which leads south, about 6 miles, up to Sierra Madre Road and the ridge.

Aliso Park Campground
U.S. Forest Service

GENERAL SETTING (LOCATION, FEATURES, SUPPLIES, INFORMATION) Scattered oaks on golden hills create a scene here that is familiar in Southern California's inland valleys. This scenery occurs a few miles south of Highway 166, as the rolling terrain of the open range leads toward the foothills of the Sierra Madre Mountains. Watch out for cattle crossing the roads.

This primitive campground is located in Aliso Canyon, southwest of New Cuyama, in the greater Cuyama Valley area. Its setting, in a well-shaded glen of tall oaks, gives it the appearance of a woodland park, making it desirable for day-use picnicking as well as overnight camping. The elevation here is 3200 feet.

Of the two hiking trails that begin at the southern end of camp, only the easternmost trail is discussed here. This rather lengthy and steep trail, of roughly 5 miles, connects the camp with the Sierra Madre Ridge. The trail leads southwest and partly follows Aliso Canyon, thick with chaparral and oaks, then passes by Hog Pen Spring, the location of an old trail camp. On Sierra Madre Ridge, the trail ends at Sierra Madre Road (32S13), which is open to hikers, but closed to vehicles, east of McPherson Peak.

Gasoline and limited supplies are available in New Cuyama, on Highway 166, 2.5 miles east of Aliso Canyon Road. A sign there says NEXT SERVICES 54 MILES (in Santa Maria, west). Supplies are also available in Taft and Maricopa, roughly 35 miles northeast.

For more information, write or phone the Mount Pinos Ranger District of the Los Padres National Forest.

SITES, FEES, FACILITIES, RESTRICTIONS There are 10 dirt sites for tents or RVs. A parked vehicle requires an Adventure Pass (fee) for overnight camping or day use (picnicking, hiking, etc.).

Each site has one or more picnic tables (up to three) and a steel fire ring with grill. The camp has two centrally located vault toilets, but no water or hookups. RVs must be self-contained.

The camp and roads are usually open, but are subject to closure during rains or fires. *Caution:* roads near camp are poorly paved, rough, and have some potholes. Camping limit is 14 days. Sites are nonreservable. Maximum RV length is 22 feet. Fires are permitted only in the camp's fire rings. Dogs must be leashed.

DIRECTIONS From the intersection of State Highways 166 and 33, southwest of Maricopa, take State Highway 166 west. Go about 10.5 miles, and New Cuyama is reached (a supply point). Then continue on Highway 166 about 2.5 miles farther to Aliso Canyon Road. Turn left (south) and go about 4 miles to Foothill Road, just beyond the oil field tanks. Turn right (west), and after going about 1.5 miles, the road bends south and its name changes to Aliso Park Road. Go about a mile to the road's end and the camp.

Ventura County

Ventura County has 1863 square miles of spectacular scenery within its borders and ranks 27th in size among California's 58 counties (Santa Barbara County, with 2737 square miles, ranks 22nd). Its coastline, which faces the Channel Islands about 30 miles offshore, is approximately 50 miles long. The ten public campgrounds along its length are among some of the most interesting beach campgrounds in Southern California. Rincon Parkway Campground, for example, is located about as close to the ocean as one can get and still stay dry. Camping sites are on the immediate landward side of the sea wall that forms the oceanside boundary of Pacific Coast Highway (old Rincon Highway). Rincon is also one of the more famous surfing spots on the coast.

Most of the county is mountainous, the mountains being part of the Transverse Range. Mount Pinos, in the northern section of the county, is adjacent to Mount Pinos Campground and has an elevation of 8831 feet. Reyes Peak in the county's central section is adjacent to Reyes Peak Campground and has an elevation of 7510 feet. The county has two large fresh-water lakes, Lake Piru and Lake Casitas, featuring fishing and water sports. Public campgrounds are adjacent to both lakes.

Places to see and visit are numerous. Ventura features several fine museums, and several antique shops are found in the downtown area. The picturesque town of Ojai with its unique shops lies just a short distance inland from Ventura. Two fine yacht harbors, Ventura Harbor with its Channel Islands National Park Visitor Center, and Channel Islands Harbor near Port Hueneme, are close by McGrath State Beach and Campground. Both harbors feature fine-dining restaurants. Transportation to the Channel Islands can be arranged at Ventura Harbor. Tours of the U.S. Naval Construction Battalion Center and its harbor at Port Hueneme, and the Point Mugu Naval Weapons Center can be arranged. The small harbor at Port Hueneme was one of the busiest on the Pacific Coast during World War II. Most of the equipment supporting the famous Sea Bees in WWII and Korea was shipped from this harbor. The Ronald Reagan Presidential Library is located in Simi Valley. Tours may be arranged.

Campgrounds in Kern County which are in close proximity to the northern border of Ventura County have been included.

VENTURA COUNTY
COASTAL AREA CAMPGROUNDS

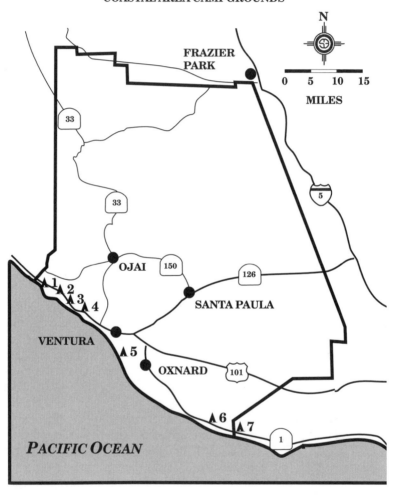

VENTURA COUNTY
COASTAL AREA

Emma Wood State Beach

Hobson County Park
Ventura County Parks

GENERAL SETTING (LOCATION, FEATURES, SUPPLIES, IN-FORMATION) A few palm trees lend a tropical touch to this coastal park located about halfway between Ventura and Carpinteria. Some sites sit about 10 feet above the beach and have ocean views. Coastal hills form a dramatic backdrop. Swimming, surfing, and surf fishing (license required) are popular. The park features a store and snack bar, two day-use picnic tables at the store, and a day-use parking lot. A camp host resides next to the store.

Supplies are available at the park store (phone for hours) and in Ventura. For more information, contact Ventura County Parks.

SITES, FEES, FACILITIES, RESTRICTIONS There are 31 numbered sites for tents or RVs, with up to 6 people per site. From April 1 to October 31, the nightly fee is $20 per site, and from November 1 to March 31, the nightly fee is $17 per site. There are dirt-and-gravel sites and spurs. Reservations are $5 per site.

Each site has a picnic table and a steel fire ring with grill. The restroom has sinks, flush toilets, a laundry sink, and wheelchair access. There are indoor hot (pay) showers near the restroom, outdoor cold showers near the beach, a drinking fountain, soft drink and newspaper vending machines, pay phones, an information board, a bicycle rack, trash cans, a dumpster, and a recycling bin.

The park is usually open. Camping limit is 14 days. Maximum RV length is 34 feet. For fires, use only the park's fire rings. Dogs must be leashed. The nightly fee is $1 per dog.

DIRECTIONS From central Ventura, take U.S. Highway 101 northwest about 1.5 miles to the State Beaches exit (Pacific Coast Highway). Go about 6 miles to the park.

Rincon Parkway Campground
Ventura County Parks

GENERAL SETTING (LOCATION, FEATURES, SUPPLIES, IN-FORMATION) For those who like no-frills beach camping, this is the place to stay. It resembles some camping areas in the desert, with one major advantage—it has the ocean at its doorstep. This primitive camping area for RVs is located along a one-mile stretch of the Rincon Parkway, between Hobson and Faria County Parks.

The camping area consists of sand-and-gravel RV parking spaces on the road's southbound parking lane. All sites are on the ocean side of the road, separated from the ocean by a sea wall. There is not much beach beyond the wall. The parkway rises about 10 to 12 feet above the ocean. The ocean affords plenty of surf fishing opportunities (license required). Beach residences can be seen at various points along the road, near the camping area. Day-use-only parking spaces are located south of Faria County Park. Supplies are available in Ventura, 8 miles southeast, via Highway 101. For more information, contact Ventura County Parks.

SITES, FEES, FACILITIES, RESTRICTIONS The parkway has 115 nonreservable, sand-and-gravel sites for RVs (no hookups). From April 1 to October 31, the nightly fee is $16 per site, and from November 1 to March 31, the nightly fee is $13 per site.

The fee includes one RV and one automobile per site. An automobile may not be parked overnight without an RV. An additional vehicle is charged the full nightly fee. The camping and day-use areas have portable toilets, dumpsters, recycling bins, and information boards with fees and rules. There is no water.

The parkway is usually open. Camping limit is 5 days, April 1 to October 31, and 10 days, November 1 to March 31. Maximum RV length is 34 feet. Cooking fires are permitted in commercially built stoves. Dogs must be leashed. The nightly fee is $1 per dog.

DIRECTIONS From central Ventura, take U.S. Highway 101 northwest about 1.5 miles to the State Beaches exit (Pacific Coast Highway). Go half a mile to the day-use area and 4 miles to camp.

Faria County Park
Ventura County Parks

GENERAL SETTING (LOCATION, FEATURES, SUPPLIES, INFORMATION) Monterey cypress trees and palms provide limited shade but give this ocean park a California beach atmosphere. Santa Cruz Island and other islands provide a striking view. The local coastal area resembles typical Mediterranean coastlines with their offshore islands. The park is northwest of Ventura, near the residential communities of Solimar Beach and Faria Beach.

The park features a playground, horseshoe pits, benches, and a park store with snack bar. Surfing and surf fishing is available in the ocean (license required). A camp host resides next to the park store. A day-use parking lot is provided. Supplies are available at the park store (phone for hours) and in Ventura. For more information, contact Ventura County Parks.

SITES, FEES, FACILITIES, RESTRICTIONS There are 42 numbered, dirt-and-gravel sites, for tents or RVs, with up to six people per site. Four sites have full hookups. Fees per site, per night follow. For full-hookup sites, year-round, the fee is $30. For non-hookup sites, from April 1 to October 31, the fee is $20, and from November 1 to March 31, the fee is $17. Sites are reservable, and the reservation fee is $5 per site. Some sites have level, paved parking spurs and are wheelchair accessible.

Each site has a picnic table and a steel fire ring with grill. The restroom has sinks, flush toilets, a laundry sink, and wheelchair access. There are indoor hot (pay) showers near the restroom, outdoor cold showers near the beach, a drinking fountain, pay phones, an information board, trash cans, a dumpster, and a recycling bin. Vending machines dispense ice, soft drinks, and newspapers.

The park is usually open. Camping limit is 14 days. Maximum RV length is 34 feet. Fires are allowed only in the park's fire rings. Dogs must be leashed. The nightly fee is $1 per dog.

DIRECTIONS From central Ventura, take U.S. Highway 101 northwest about 1.5 miles to the State Beaches exit (Pacific Coast Highway). Go about 4 miles to the park.

Emma Wood State Beach
North Beach Campground
Ventura River Group Camp

GENERAL SETTING (LOCATION, FEATURES, SUPPLIES, INFORMATION) Emma Wood State Beach consists of two campgrounds near each other. North Beach Camp has individual sites set on a bare strip along a low bluff between the camp road and the beach. The sites have ocean views. Ventura River Group Camp is situated near where the river meets the sea. It features two nature trails, a bicycle path, and a picnic area.

Nearby San Buenaventura State Beach is an enjoyable day-use area. It has a beach with lifeguard service during spring and summer, a volleyball court on the sand, a bicycle path, a picnic area on the lawn, a summer snack bar, and a large parking lot. In Ventura, take U.S. Highway 101 to the Seaward Avenue exit. Turn

west, and at Harbor Boulevard, turn north. Go a short way to San
Pedro Street, turn west, and go to the entrance (fee: see below).
Nearby historic downtown Ventura is the location of Mission
San Buenaventura and Ventura County Museum of History and
Art. Surf fishing is available in the ocean (license required).
Supplies are available in the downtown Ventura area. For more
information, write or phone Emma Wood State Beach.

SITES, FEES, FACILITIES, RESTRICTIONS North Beach
Campground has 97 individual, nonreservable, numbered sites (no
hookups). The fee is $15 per site, per night, and includes one vehi-
cle and up to eight people. The nightly fee for an additional vehicle is $5. Of the sites, 19 are for overflow camping at the southern
end of camp. All sites are primitive, dirt and sand, with blacktop
spurs. There are two primitive group sites for $75 each, per night.

North Beach has portable chemical toilets, trash cans, and
dumpsters. Newspaper vending machines and a pay phone are
located at the entrance station. Some sites have blacktop spurs.
Registered campers may use the RV dump station at McGrath
State Beach, about 7 miles south, via Harbor Boulevard.

Ventura River Group Camp has five group sites (no hookups).
There is one primitive group site for RVs that takes up to 50 people and 20 vehicles, for $125 nightly. There are four developed
group sites for tent camping, each of which takes up to 30 people
and five vehicles, for $45 nightly, per site. The four tent sites may
be reserved together, for up to 120 people and 20 vehicles (5 vehicles per site), for $180 nightly. Each group site requires at least 10
people and at least one adult for every 15 youths under 18 years.
The reservation fee is $7.50 per group site.

The group camp and picnic area have picnic tables, pedestal
barbecues, drinking fountains, and restrooms with sinks and flush
toilets. The camp has piped water and an outdoor cold shower.

San Buenaventura State Beach has more than 150 picnic sites,
each with a table and barbecue. There are drinking fountains, restrooms, and a large parking lot. The day-use fee is $5 per vehicle.

Swimming is not recommended in the Emma Wood area because ocean currents tend to be strong, and no lifeguard is on duty.

Note: Ventura River Group Camp has been temporarily closed
due to storm damage. Both camps are usually open otherwise, but
are subject to closure during rainy weather. Camping limit at individual sites is 7 days, June to September, and 15 days, October
to May. Limit at group sites is seven days, all year. Quiet time is

from 10 P.M. to 6 A.M. Maximum RV length is 35 feet. Confine fires
to the state beaches' barbecues and fire rings. Dogs must be leashed
and kept away from the beach. The nightly fee is $1 per dog.

DIRECTIONS From central Ventura, take Main Street a short
way northwest. Just beyond the Ventura River, bear left (southwest) on the access road and go to Ventura River Group Camp.
If the road to North Beach is closed, take U.S. Highway 101
northwest from central Ventura about 1.5 miles to the State Beaches exit (Pacific Coast Highway). Go half a mile to North Beach.

McGrath State Beach

**GENERAL SETTING (LOCATION, FEATURES, SUPPLIES,
INFORMATION)** McGrath State Beach, located between Ventura and Oxnard, contains nearly 300 acres, at an elevation of just 5
feet. Rounded myoprom trees afford privacy and some shade in
camp. Low-lying sand dunes separate the camp from the beach,
and along with the trees, hide the view. From the beach the Channel Islands can be seen; they enhance the ocean view to the west.

The state beach has a tree-shaded campfire center with benches, and a visitor center near the entrance (open limited hours). A
nature trail leads through a natural preserve that is a sanctuary
for marine birds. Surf fishing is popular (license required).

Visit the mission and Ventura County Museum of History and
Art are in Ventura, about 4 miles north. Channel Islands Harbor,
about 5 miles south in Oxnard, has a New England style.

Supplies are available in Ventura and Oxnard. A camp host
resides in the camping area and sells firewood. For more information, phone or write McGrath State Beach.

SITES, FEES, FACILITIES, RESTRICTIONS There are 174
developed sites for tents or RVs (no hookups). Fees per site, per
night, follow. From March 15 to September 15, the fee is $18 on
Friday and Saturday, and $17 on other nights. From September
16 to March 14, the fee is $14 on every night. The fee includes one
vehicle and up to eight persons per site. The nightly fee for an
additional vehicle is $5. Senior citizens get a $2 discount on fees
for all sites except hike and bike sites. Reservations are required
on summer weekends and major holidays, and are $7.50 per site.

The campground has dirt and grass campsites, paved parking
spurs and roads, and some wheelchair access.

Each site has a picnic table and a steel fire ring with grill. The camp has water spigots and wheelchair-accessible restrooms with sinks, hot (pay) showers, flush toilets, and outdoor laundry sinks. Drinking fountains and a soft drink vending machine are at the central restroom. Newspaper vending machines and pay phones are at the entrance. There are trash cans, dumpsters, a recycling bin, and an RV water station and dump station. The day-use fee, per vehicle, is $5 for parking or for use of the dump station.

The hike and bike camping area has 10 sites. The fee is $3 per person, per night. Each site has a picnic table and a fire ring. A bicycle rack is provided. Restrooms with flush toilets are nearby.

The state beach is usually open, but is subject to closure during rainy weather. Camping limit is 7 days, June to September, and 15 days, October to May. Check-in is at 2 P.M., and check-out is at 12 noon. Quiet hours are from 10 P.M. to 6 A.M. Ocean swimming is not recommended because of heavy currents. Extra-vehicle parking is limited. Maximum length for trailers is 30 feet, and for motorhomes and campers, 34 feet. Fires are permitted only in the state beach's fire rings. Dogs must be leashed and kept away from the preserve and the beach. The nightly fee is $1 per dog.

DIRECTIONS From U.S. 101 in Ventura, exit at Seaward Avenue. Turn west, toward the ocean, and at Harbor Boulevard, turn south. Go about 3 miles to the entrance road, and turn west.

Point Mugu State Park
Thornhill Broome Beach Campground
Sycamore Canyon Campground
La Jolla Group Camp

GENERAL SETTING (LOCATION, FEATURES, SUPPLIES, INFORMATION) Point Mugu State Park includes three campgrounds and is located about midway between Malibu and Ventura, at sea level. The park's nearly 15,000 acres reach northeast from the Pacific Ocean into the Santa Monica Mountains, toward the city limits of Thousand Oaks. Trails for hiking, horseback riding, and bicycling have been developed in the hills. The day-use picnic area is located next to the beach near Sycamore Canyon Camp. Surf fishing is permitted (license required). Swimmers are strongly cautioned there are riptides in the ocean, and lifeguard service is limited.

Thornhill Broome Beach Campground is set along a sandy beach with no trees, so the camp has an unobstructed view of the ocean and neighboring coastline. This includes a view of the huge Point Mugu rock, to the northwest, roughly a mile away. The coast highway passes between this rock and the coastal cliffs. Winds are strong at Thornhill Broome Beach, as can be seen by the sand piled up against the foothills across the highway. Campsites have been placed along the paved camp road that is parallel to the coast highway, on the beach side. These campsites are RV parking spaces on the southbound side of the camp road. Each space is parallel to the road and next to its campsite on the beach sand.

Sycamore Canyon Campground is set in a coastal canyon near Big Sycamore Canyon Trail. Oaks and sycamores shade some sites, and chaparral affords privacy. A camp host resides in camp. Nearby Sycamore Cove Picnic Area and Sycamore Canyon Ranger Station are next to the beach. Myoprom trees partly shade the picnic area. For day-use fees and picnic facilities, see below.

La Jolla Group Camp, in the coastal hills, has a feeling of remoteness, yet is not far from the coast highway. It sits at a trailhead in a canyon of chaparral. The trail wanders into the hills and is for equestrians and hikers, but not dogs, bicycles, or other vehicles. Ray Miller Trailhead is at the end of La Jolla Canyon Road, just north of the turnoff to the group camp. The plaque at the trailhead says Ray Miller was the "First official California State Park camp host volunteer." The trailhead has a small picnic area in a sycamore grove. For facilities and the day-use fee, see below.

Supplies are available in Oxnard, about 12 miles northwest, via Highway 1. The store at Leo Carrillo State Beach carries limited supplies and is open during summer; phone for hours. For more information, write or phone Point Mugu State Park.

SITES, FEES, FACILITIES, RESTRICTIONS Thornhill Broome Beach Campground has 102 individual, primitive , numbered sites (no hookups). Fees per site, per night are as follows. From March 1 to November 30, the fee is $11 on Friday and Saturday, and $10 on other nights. From December 1 to February 28, the fee is $7 on every night. Each site has a picnic table and a steel fire ring (with grill) or a concrete barbecue. The camp has water spigots, cold showers, and portable chemical toilets, a few of which have wheelchair access. Trash cans and dumpsters are provided. Two pay phones are located near the entrance.

Sycamore Canyon Campground has 57 individual, developed, numbered sites (no hookups). Fees per site, per night are as follows. From March 1 to November 30, the fee is $18 on Friday and Saturday, and $17 on other nights. From December 1 to February 28, the fee is $14 on every night. The day-use fee is $6 ($5 for senior citizens). Each campsite has a picnic table and a steel fire ring with grill. Wheelchair-accessible restrooms have a drinking fountain, hot (pay) showers, flush toilets, outdoor wash basins, and laundry sinks. The camp has water spigots, an RV dump station, dumpsters, a recycling bin, an information board, and blacktop parking spurs. Pay phones are located near the entrance. Phone the park for information on hike and bike sites.

The individual site fee includes one vehicle and up to eight people per site. The nightly fee for an additional vehicle is $6. Senior citizens receive a $2 discount on fees for all individual sites except hike and bike sites.

La Jolla Group Camp has one developed, walk-in, group campsite for $75 per night. Only tent camping is permitted (no RVs). No more than 50 people and 16 vehicles are allowed. There are 16 parking spaces, and no camping is permitted in the dirt parking area. The walk from this parking area to the campsite is about 1000 feet. Anyone 17 years of age or younger must be accompanied by an adult. The group site has water spigots, three picnic tables, two large pedestal barbecues, a steel fire ring (with grill), and a picnic shelter (ramada). The wheelchair-accessible restroom has a drinking fountain, flush toilets, outdoor wash basins, and laundry sinks. A hitching post and trash cans are provided.

Sycamore Cove Picnic Area has about 50 individual picnic sites. The day-use fee is $6 per vehicle ($5 for senior citizens). Each picnic site has a picnic table and a concrete barbecue. The group picnic site has several tables, concrete barbecues, and water spigots. The picnic area has water spigots, wheelchair-accessible restrooms, trash cans, dumpsters, paved parking area, and pay phones.

Most campsites are reservable, and reservations are $7.50 per site. Reservations are required for groups at the picnic area (fee).

Ray Miller Trailhead has a small picnic area with a few tables, a drinking fountain, water spigot, trash cans, an information board, and a small parking lot. The day-use fee is $2 per vehicle.

Point Mugu State park is usually open, but is subject to closure during rains or fires. Camping limit at individual campsites is 7 days, June to September, and 15 days, October to May. Camping limit at the group campsite is seven days, year-round. The park observes quiet time from 10 P.M. to 6 A.M. Parking is limited. Maximum length for trailers, motorhomes, and campers is 31 feet. No fires are permitted except in the state beach's fire rings. No gathering of wood is permitted. Dogs must be leashed. The nightly fee is $1 per dog.

DIRECTIONS From the junction of State Highways 1 and 34 in Oxnard, take State Highway 1 southeast about 12.5 miles to *Thornhill Broome Beach Camp*, on the beach side of the road. Continue about a quarter mile to La Jolla Canyon Road. Turn left and go about a quarter mile. At the turnoff to La Jolla Group Camp, turn right and go a short distance to the parking area. Walk about 1000 feet to *La Jolla Group Camp*. Ray Miller Trailhead is at the end of La Jolla Canyon Road, beyond La Jolla Group Camp turnoff.

Back on Highway 1, continue southeast about 1.5 miles to Sycamore Canyon Ranger Station and Sycamore Cove Picnic Area, on the beach side of the road. To the left is the side road that leads about a quarter mile north to *Sycamore Canyon Campground*.

Leo Carrillo State Beach

GENERAL SETTING (LOCATION, FEATURES, SUPPLIES, INFORMATION) This 1600-acre state beach is located just east of Ventura County and so is included in this book. The campground is situated back in the hills, away from the beach, in the Arroyo Sequit, a wide canyon. Eucalyptus trees, sycamore trees, and chaparral create a scene of rustic beauty and partly shade the sites. The campfire center at the camp's north end features a stage, benches, and a fire ring. Hiking trails lead into the coastal hills.

There is beach access, and activities include surfing, windsurfing, beach walking, and fishing (license required). Swimmers are cautioned that lifeguards are on duty during summer only.

Limited supplies are available at the state beach store within the canyon camping area. This store is open during summer; phone for hours. Supplies are available in Malibu, 16 miles east, via State Highway 1. For more information, contact Leo Carrillo State Beach.

SITES, FEES, FACILITIES, RESTRICTIONS There are 140 individual, developed sites for RVs or tents. Fees per site, per night are as follows. From March 1 to November 30, the fee is $18 on Friday and Saturday, and $17 on other nights. From December 1 to February 28, the fee is $14 on every night. The fee includes a maximum of eight persons and one vehicle per site. The nightly fee for an additional vehicle is $6. The camp has dirt and grass sites and blacktop spurs. A camp host resides in camp. Each site has a picnic table and a steel fire ring with grill. The camp has water spigots, an RV water station, and a dump station. Wheelchair-accessible restrooms have a drinking fountain, hot (pay) showers, sinks, flush toilets, and a laundry sink. Pay phones, two newspaper vending machines, a soft drink vending machine, and two picnic tables are located at the state beach store in camp. Trash cans, dumpsters, and recycling bins are provided.

The primitive group site for tents (not RVs) is at the north end of camp near the campfire center. The nightly fee of $75 includes a maximum of 50 people and 16 vehicles. These vehicles must be parked in the parking lot that is next to the campfire center and is across the camp road from the group site. No camping is permitted in the parking lot. A restroom and pay phone are nearby. Anyone 17 years old or younger must have a parent's written consent.

Most sites are reservable, and reservations are $7.50 per site. Senior citizens receive a $2 discount on fees at all individual sites except hike and bike sites. The day-use fee is $6 per vehicle ($5 for seniors). The day-use beach area has restrooms and a parking lot.

The hike and bike camp area has five sites, each with a table and fire ring, for $3 per person, per night. A restroom is nearby.

Note: heavy storms wiped out the old beach area campsites, and future plans for that area are indefinite, as of this writing.

The canyon camping area is usually open, but is subject to closure during rains or fires. Camping limit at individual sites is 7 days, June to September, and 15 days, October to May. Limit at the group site is seven days, year-round. Quiet time is from 10 P.M. to 6 A.M. Maximum length for trailers, motorhomes, and campers is 31 feet. Maximum height for all vehicles accessing the beach is 8 feet, because of the low-clearance underpass. Fires are permitted only in the state beach's fire rings. Dogs must be leashed and kept away from the beach. The fee is $1 per dog, per night.

DIRECTIONS From central Malibu, take State Highway 1 (Pacific Coast Highway) west about 16 miles to the Leo Carrillo State Beach access road (just before reaching Mulholland Highway). Turn right (north) and go a short way to the entrance.

VENTURA COUNTY
INLAND VALLEY AREA CAMPGROUNDS

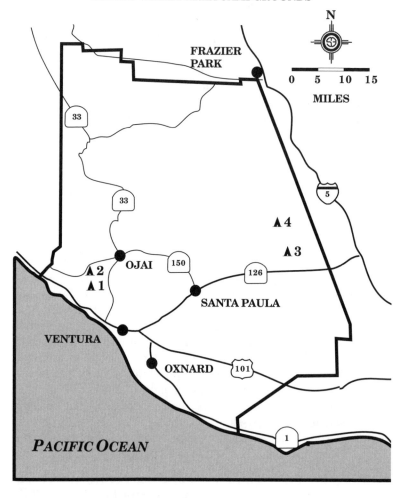

VENTURA COUNTY INLAND VALLEY AREA

▲1 Foster County Park
▲2 Lake Casitas Recreation Area
▲3 Lake Piru Recreation Area
▲4 Blue Point

Lake Casitas Recreation Area

Foster County Park
Ventura County Parks

GENERAL SETTING (LOCATION, FEATURES, SUPPLIES, IN-FORMATION) This county park is located in the Ventura River Valley, nearly midway between the Ventura coastal area and the Ojai Valley, and is within 10 miles of both. Sparsely wooded hills on the valley's east side contrast with hills covered in chaparral and oaks on the west side.

The park is situated on a slightly inclined slope that is partly shaded by oak trees. It features a playground and a horseshoe pit. The climate is pleasant most of the year due to the valley's proximity to the ocean. A camp host resides in the campground.

Ojai offers many diversions while you are in this area, including a museum, art galleries, golf, and hiking.

Supplies are available in Ventura, about 7 miles south, and in Ojai, about 8 miles north. For more information, write or phone Ventura County Parks.

SITES, FEES, FACILITIES, RESTRICTIONS The park has 21 nonreservable, numbered campsites for tents or RVs (no hookups). From April 1 to October 31, the nightly fee is $14 per site. From November 1 to March 31, the nightly fee is $11 per site. A maximum of six people are allowed at each site. Some campsites have dirt spurs; other sites have room to park on the dirt. The park has paved camp roads.

Each site has a picnic table. Most sites have either a steel fire ring (with grill) or a small concrete barbecue. The park has water spigots, drinking fountains, a restroom with sinks and flush toilets, trash cans, and a dumpster. A pay phone and an information board are located at the entrance.

The park is usually open, except during fires or inclement weather. Camping limit is 14 days. Maximum RV length is 34 feet. Fires are permitted only in the park's barbecues and fire rings. Dogs must be leashed. The nightly fee is $1 per dog.

DIRECTIONS From U.S. Highway 101 in Ventura, take State Highway 33 north about 7 miles to the Casitas Vista Road exit. When you exit, the off-ramp takes you to Ventura Avenue. Turn right (south), go about a tenth mile, and at Casitas Vista Road, turn right (west). Go about a quarter mile to the park entrance on the left (south) side of the road.

Lake Casitas Recreation Area
Casitas Municipal Water District

GENERAL SETTING (LOCATION, FEATURES, SUPPLIES, INFORMATION) The chaparral-covered coastal hills provide the backdrop for this stunning 6200-acre park and lake in the western Ojai Valley. It is a popular place for families and kids to relax and play, with 12 campgrounds and over 450 campsites, 13 picnic areas, fishing and boating areas on the lake, horseshoe pits, horse-drawn carriage rides, a model airstrip, and seven playgrounds, the largest being near the entrance. The camps and picnic areas are situated fairly close together on the lake's north side, so are not treated separately. Oaks, pines, sycamores, pepper trees, and eucalyptus trees shade portions of the recreation area.

Ojai is the area's focal point for art and craft galleries, antique shops, farmers' markets, a wide variety of restaurants, botanical gardens, golf, hiking, and more. The Ojai Valley Museum tops it all off. Ojai is about 6 miles east of Lake Casitas via Highway 150.

Lake Casitas is a great spot for fishing (license required) and boating (fee). The lake contains bass and sunfish, and is stocked with trout and catfish from October to May. Boats can be rented, including motor boats, row boats, canoes, kayaks, paddle boats, and patio deck boats. The lake features a marina, fishing docks, launch ramps, boat slips, fish-cleaning sinks, and garbage disposals. Fishing licenses, fuel, tackle, and bait are available.

A first-aid station is located near the entrance. Some campgrounds and picnic areas have views of the lake. Bicycle trails are provided, and bicycles can be rented near the entrance. Monthly rental storage for boats and trailers is available. Park hosts and rangers are usually present to answer questions.

The park store carries groceries, ice, wood, charcoal, and propane. It is open every day, April 15 to September 15, but has limited hours otherwise. The snack bar and the bait and tackle shop are located on the camp road near the eastern boat ramp, south of the entrance. The snack bar is open year-round. Ice, bait, and limited supplies are also carried at a local market (see Directions). Supplies are also available in Ojai. For more information, write or phone Lake Casitas Recreation Area.

SITES, FEES, FACILITIES, RESTRICTIONS There are 21 full-hookup sites, 141 partial-hookup sites (electricity and water), and about 300 non-hookup sites. These individual (or family) sites are numbered and divided among 12 campgrounds. Some hookup sites have paved, level spurs and are wheelchair accessible.

Nightly fees, per site, are as follows, and are subject to change. Executive full-hookup sites each have a concrete parking spur with a small lawn area, for $39.75. Deluxe partial-hookup sites each have a concrete spur with a small lawn area (but no sewer hookups), for $34.50. Basic partial-hookup sites (without concrete spur or lawn) are $19.50 from November 1 to February 28, and $21.50 the rest of the year. Premium basic non-hookup sites have a view and are $15 from November 1 to February 28, and $17 the rest of the year. Basic, primitive non-hookup sites (without view) are $15. Some fees are higher on major holidays; phone for details.

The fee includes one vehicle and up to six persons per site. The nightly fee for a second vehicle is $9.50. Reservations are recommended every day during summer and weekends the rest of the year. The reservation fee is $6 per individual (family) site.

Each individual (family) site has a picnic table and a steel fire ring with grill. Each camp has water spigots and trash cans. Some camps have full-scale, wheelchair-accessible restrooms with sinks, flush toilets, and hot (pay) showers. Other camps have RV-style pedal-flush toilets, vault toilets, or portable chemical toilets. Some pedal-flush toilets are wheelchair accessible.

The nightly fee for group camping is $16 per vehicle, with a minimum of 10 vehicles per group, and a reservation fee of $60.

Group camping areas have picnic tables, a rock fire pit (bonfire pit), benches, water spigots, and toilets nearby.

Lake Casitas Recreation Area has two RV dump stations. Pay phones are located near the entrance and at the park store. A newspaper vending machine is at the store. Dumpsters, trash cans, and recycling bins are provided throughout the recreation area.

Picnic areas have picnic tables, pedestal barbecues or fire rings, a picnic shelter (shade ramada), various toilet facilities, and trash cans. Some picnic areas have paved parking lots; others have dirt parking areas. Group picnic sites have picnic tables, a large barbecue, a ramada, and a horseshoe pit.

The day-use fee is $6.50 per motor vehicle. Phone for information on reduced-fee permits for frequent day use. The fee for group picnic reservations is $100.

The recreation area is usually open. Camping limit is 14 days. Check-out is at 2 P.M. Quiet hours are from 10 P.M. to 7 A.M.

No swimming, water-skiing, or jet skiing is permitted, because the lake is a drinking water source. Maximum length for RVs is 40 feet. The speed limit is 5 m.p.h. in camps and 15 m.p.h. on park roads. Permissible boat length is 11 to 24 feet. Fires are permitted only in the recreation area's barbecues and fire rings. Dogs must be leashed and kept 50 feet away from the lake's shoreline. The nightly camping fee is $2 per dog; the day-use fee is $1 per dog.

DIRECTIONS From Ventura, take State Highway 33 north about 10 miles to Santa Ana Boulevard in Oak View. Turn left (west) and go about a mile to Santa Ana Road. A market on the corner carries limited supplies. Turn right (north) and go about 2.5 miles to the entrance station, just south of State Highway 150.

Lake Piru Recreation Area
United Water Conservation District

GENERAL SETTING (LOCATION, FEATURES, SUPPLIES, INFORMATION) This recreation area is located in wide Piru Canyon, north of Piru and northwest of Valencia. The United Water Conservation District operates the recreation area and built Santa Felicia Dam across Piru Creek in 1955, creating Lake Piru. Hydro-power, irrigation, water conservation, and flood control are among the lake's many uses. There are over 200 individual sites, two group sites, a shaded picnic area on a lawn, and a playground. Individual sites are divided between Olive Grove and Oak Lane camps, also referred to as Olive Tree and Oaks camps, adjacent to each other at the southwest end of the lake. The names indicate the type of tree that shades each camp. The elevation is 1000 feet.

Boating, water-skiing, and fishing are permitted on the lake, stocked with trout, and bass, catfish, and sunfish can also be caught (license required). The lake features a marina, rental pontoon boats and fishing boats, a free boat launch ramp, a dock, boat slips, and a fish-cleaning area. Bait, tackle, and boat fuel are available.

Swimming is permitted only at the designated beach area. Lifeguard service is provided in summer. No jet skis are allowed.

The marina store and snack bar carries ice and limited supplies. Supplies are also available in Valencia. For more information, write or phone Lake Piru Recreation Area.

SITES, FEES, FACILITIES, RESTRICTIONS Individual site fees, per vehicle, per night, payable in advance, follow. Olive Grove has 5 RV sites with full hookups for $23, 101 RV sites with electrical hookups for $20, and 95 sites for tents or RVs (no hookups) for $17. Oak Lane has 38 sites for tents or RVs (no hookups) for $17. There are blacktop roads and numbered, dirt-and-gravel sites.

The nightly camping fee includes one vehicle and up to four people per site. Fees are $1 higher on holidays. The fee for each additional person is $2. One additional car is permitted per campsite for $7.50, if owned by a spouse or unmarried child living in the parent's home. The fee for a vehicle towed in is $7.50 but does not apply to a motorhome towing a vehicle.

Each individual site has one or two picnic tables and a steel fire ring with grill. There are water spigots, drinking fountains, trash cans, and two RV dump stations. Restrooms have sinks, hot showers, flush toilets, and wheelchair access. One restroom at Olive Grove also has pay washing machines and a laundry sink. A soft drink vending machine is available nearby. Pay phones are located at the entrance and at the marina.

The drive-in group site is just east of Oak Lane Camp. The walk-in group site is east of the day-use group picnic area. The nightly group fee is $17 per vehicle. Group camping requires a stay of at least two nights, an occupancy of at least 4 but up to 12 units, a key deposit of $10, and a reservation fee of $20 plus a transaction fee of $5. Group campsites have picnic tables, barbecues or fire rings, vault toilets, trash cans, and parking areas.

The day-use fee is $7.50 for each vehicle, motorcycle, and private boat. The picnic area has drinking fountains, picnic tables, pedestal barbecues, shade ramadas, vault toilets, trash cans, and a parking lot. The group picnic section, for up to 120 people, can be reserved for special events, for a fee of $25 plus a cleaning deposit of $100. The day-use fee for use of the RV dump station is $3.

Olive Grove Camp is usually open. Oak Lane Camp and the group sites are open from April to October. Camping limit is 14 days. Check-out is at 2 P.M. Quiet time is from 10 P.M. to 8 A.M. Maximum RV length is 16 feet. The speed limit is 5 m.p.h. Fires are permitted only in the recreation area's barbecues and fire rings. Minimum boat length is 12 feet. Dogs must be leashed and kept out of the water. The nightly fee or day-use fee is $1 per pet.

DIRECTIONS From I-5, just north of Valencia, take State Highway 126 west about 12 miles to Main Street in Piru. Turn right (north) and go about 6.5 miles to the entrance. (Main Street becomes Piru Canyon Road, north of Piru.)

Blue Point Campground
U.S. Forest Service

GENERAL SETTING (LOCATION, FEATURES, SUPPLIES, INFORMATION) Named for a natural prominence on a local hill, this campground is located on Piru Creek, roughly 7 miles north of Lake Piru. Lake Piru offers fishing for trout, bass, and catfish (license required). Forest Road 4N13 continues north from the camp and is open to hiking but closed to motor vehicles. It leads about a mile north to Agua Blanca Trail (19W10) which goes northwest into the Sespe Wilderness; phone for regulations.

Supplies are available in Valencia. The marina store at Lake Piru Recreation Area carries ice and some supplies.

For more information, phone Lake Piru Recreation Area, which runs the campground for the U.S. Forest Service, or contact the Ojai Ranger District of the Los Padres National Forest.

SITES, FEES, FACILITIES, RESTRICTIONS There are 43 non-reservable sites for tents or RVs (no hookups) for $7 per site, per night. The fee includes one vehicle and up to four people per site. The nightly fee for an additional vehicle is $3.

Each site has a picnic table and a steel fire ring with grill. The camp has vault toilets but no water or hookups.

Note: this camp has been temporarily closed for the protection of endangered species. The camp and the 5-mile road leading to it were closed to motor vehicles, at the time of this writing, so facility information was not verifiable on site. The camp is usually open otherwise from May to September.

Camping limit is 14 days. Quiet time is from 10 P.M. to 8 A.M. Maximum RV length is 16 feet. For fires, use only the camp's fire rings. Dogs must be leashed.

DIRECTIONS From I-5, just north of Valencia, take State Highway 126 west about 12 miles to Main Street in Piru. Turn right (north) and go about 6.5 miles to Lake Piru Recreation Area's entrance. (Main Street becomes Piru Canyon Road, north of Piru, then becomes Forest Road 4N13 at Lake Piru.) Pay the fees and drive through the recreation area, going north about 7 miles to Blue Point Camp.

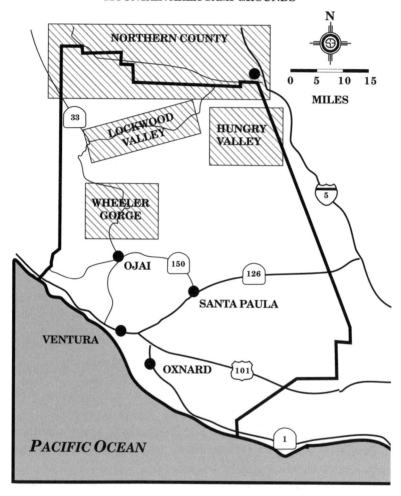

VENTURA COUNTY
MOUNTAIN AREA CAMPGROUNDS

N

0   5   10   15

MILES

NORTHERN COUNTY

33

LOCKWOOD VALLEY

HUNGRY VALLEY

5

WHEELER GORGE

OJAI

150

126

SANTA PAULA

VENTURA

OXNARD

101

1

PACIFIC OCEAN

VENTURA COUNTY
MOUNTAIN AREA

Because of the large number of public campgrounds in this area, campgrounds are grouped in four subsections by county location: Wheeler Gorge Area, Lockwood Valley Area, Northern Ventura County Area, and Hungry Valley Area.

Pine Springs Campground

VENTURA COUNTY MOUNTAIN AREA

WHEELER GORGE
AND
ADJACENT CAMPGROUNDS

▲1 Wheeler Gorge
▲2 Holiday Group
▲3 Rose Valley
▲4 Lion

▲5 Middle Lion
▲6 Piedra Blanca Corrals
　　Group
▲7 Beaver

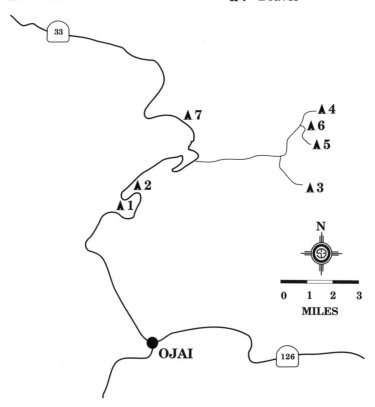

Wheeler Gorge Campground
U.S. Forest Service

GENERAL SETTING (LOCATION, FEATURES, SUPPLIES, INFORMATION) High, rocky canyon walls surround this camp set amid lush vegetation in Wheeler Gorge. The camp is located a few miles north of Wheeler Springs, northwest of Ojai. Willows, oaks, and other trees provide shade. The elevation is 2000 feet. Wheeler Gorge Nature Trail, half a mile north of camp, is a self-guided loop trail, about a mile in length, with information on chaparral, other vegetation, hawks, quails, and hummingbirds.

Ojai features art galleries, antique shops, a museum, and restaurants. Matilija Creek flows by camp and offers fishing for trout (license required). A camp host resides in camp near the entrance.

Wheeler Gorge Forest Station is across the highway, with two picnic sites. One has a picnic table and water spigot; the other has a pedestal barbecue, a steel fire ring (with grill), and a water spigot. An information board, a dumpster, and a few day-use parking spaces are set along the highway. In the Matilija Wilderness, several miles west of Wheeler Springs, a few wilderness hike-in camps are reached by lengthy hikes. Contact the Ojai Ranger District for wilderness camping information and regulations.

Supplies are available in Ojai, 9 miles southeast, via Highway 33. For more information, phone the camp host, concessionaire, or the Ojai Ranger District of the Los Padres National Forest.

SITES, FEES, FACILITIES, RESTRICTIONS There are 72 numbered sites for tents or RVs (no hookups), and 6 of these sites can be used as double sites for large families. The nightly fee is $12 per site. The limit is eight people and two vehicles per site. The nightly fee for the second vehicle is $5. Reservations are available and are $8.65 per site. Sites have blacktop spurs or dirt spurs; some are level and wheelchair accessible.

Each site has one or two picnic tables. Each site also has a pedestal barbecue or a steel fire ring (with grill), or both. The camp has water spigots, wheelchair-accessible vault toilets, dumpsters, and trash cans. A pay phone and an information board are located at the entrance. The day-use parking fee is $6 per vehicle.

The camp is usually open (except during fires, etc.). Camping limit is 14 days. Check-out is at 2 P.M. Quiet time is from 10 P.M. to 6 A.M. Maximum RV length is 16 feet. For fires, use only the camp's and picnic area's barbecues and fire rings. Dogs must be leashed.

DIRECTIONS From Ojai, take State Highway 33 north about 8 miles to camp, on the left (west) side of the road.

Holiday Group Camp
U.S. Forest Service

GENERAL SETTING (LOCATION, FEATURES, SUPPLIES, IN-FORMATION) The holiday is rather modest, but that is why rugged fans of this primitive camp keep coming back. It is set in Wheeler Gorge, north of Wheeler Springs, in a dirt clearing beside the highway, against a hill. The camp is partly shaded by scrub oak trees, and its elevation is 2000 feet. The camp host resides at Wheeler Gorge Campground, about a mile south, and sells wood.

Ortega OHV Trail (23W08), for motorcycles, is accessed on the southbound side of Highway 33, and it stretches through the hills to the northwest. Supplies are available in Ojai, 10 miles south.

For more information, phone the camp host, concessionaire, or the Ojai Ranger District of the Los Padres National Forest.

SITES, FEES, FACILITIES, RESTRICTIONS Seven scattered sites for tents or RVs (no hookups) are near a central, group cooking area. The nightly group fee is $50. Reservations are required and are $8.65 per site.

Each of the seven sites has a picnic table. Each site also has a pedestal barbecue or a steel fire ring (without grill) or both. The group cooking area has a large service table and a large brick barbecue. There are two primitive vault toilets. The water spigots are not always in service, so as a precaution, bring your own water.

The camp is usually open. Camping limit is 14 days. Quiet time is from 10 P.M. to 6 A.M. Maximum RV length is 22 feet. For fires, use the camp's barbecues and fire rings. Leash your dogs.

DIRECTIONS From Ojai, take State Highway 33 north about 9 miles to camp on the right (east) side of the road.

Rose Valley Campground
U.S. Forest Service

GENERAL SETTING (LOCATION, FEATURES, SUPPLIES, IN-FORMATION) Picturesque Rose Valley, northeast of Wheeler Springs, was named for its wild roses that bloom in the spring. Cottonwoods further enhance the valley's beauty. Rose Valley Falls, dry much of the year, is visible from camp to the southeast. It is reached by a trail that leads half a mile from camp. The camp is also referred to as Rose Valley Falls Campground, its earlier name, due to the proximity of the falls. The camp sits in a bowl-shaped clearing within the Rose Valley Recreation Area. Many trees surround the camp but few are inside it. The elevation is 3000 feet.

Three small lakes near Rose Valley Camp are stocked with trout; fishing requires a license. Vault toilets are provided at Upper and Lower Rose Valley Lakes. Forest Road 5N42, south of Rose Valley Camp, has a locked gate across it. Beyond that point, the road is for four-wheel-drive use only, and a permit is required; phone for information. This steep road leads up to Nordhoff Ridge.

Supplies are available in Ojai, 20 miles south. For more information, contact Los Padres National Forest's Ojai Ranger District.

SITES, FEES, FACILITIES, RESTRICTIONS Nine numbered nonreservable, non-hookup sites are for tents or RVs. The nightly fee is $7 per site, with up to eight people per site. Most sites have dirt and gravel spurs. Two sites are wheelchair accessible.

Each site has a picnic table, a pedestal barbecue, and a steel fire ring with grill. The camp has a wheelchair-accessible vault toilet, an information board, and trash receptacles, but no water.

This camp is usually open (closed during fires or floods). Camping limit is 14 days. Maximum RV length is 16 feet. For fires, use only the camp's barbecues and fire rings. Dogs must be leashed.

DIRECTIONS From Ojai, take State Highway 33 north 14.5 miles to Rose Valley Road (Forest Road 6N31). Turn right (east) and go 3 miles to Forest Road 5N42. Turn right (south) and go 0.5 mile.

Lion and Middle Lion Campgrounds
U.S. Forest Service

GENERAL SETTING (LOCATION, FEATURES, SUPPLIES, INFORMATION) These primitive camps are located in the Lion Canyon area within the Rose Valley Recreation Area, northeast of Wheeler Springs. Both camps' elevations are over 3000 feet. Lion Camp is of medium size, whereas Middle Lion Camp is small. Signs at the campgrounds show both camps' names in the plural, but the Forest Service's maps and website show them in the singular.

Lion Campground is in the Sespe Creek Valley, near the mouth of Lion Canyon, and is also called Lion Canyon Campground. Hills and step-like mesas to the northeast are covered in chaparral except where there are sandstone formations. Beyond these hills lies a rugged mountain skyline. The camp is spacious with spread-out campsites suitable for families. Skeletons of trees are indications of an old fire. The trees are sparse and afford little shade. A few bright green pines appear to have been transplanted.

Sespe Creek affords fishing opportunities for visitors of Lion Camp (license required). The camp is located at a major trailhead point. Hiking trails lead into the Sespe Wilderness. Piedra Blanca National Recreation Trail (22W03) leads north and northwest, and Sespe River Trail (20W14) goes east from where Rose Valley Road (Forest Road 6N31) ends. Middle Sespe Trail (22W04) goes west along the southern edge of the wilderness. Phone for information on Sespe Wilderness hike-in camps and regulations.

Middle Lion Campground is small, primitive, and resembles a remote hike-in camp. It sits on the west side of a creek where Lion Canyon and a short box canyon meet. Pines afford shade, but some trees are spindly and leafless as if there had been a fire in recent years. Surrounding hills are covered with chaparral. From Middle Lion Camp, Lion Canyon Trail (22W06) goes south along the western edge of the Sespe Wilderness. Phone for wilderness camp information and regulations. A gravel day-use parking area is provided where the road to camp meets Rose Valley Road.

Supplies are available in Ojai, 20 miles south. For more information, contact Los Padres National Forest's Ojai Ranger District.

SITES, FEES, FACILITIES, RESTRICTIONS Lion Camp has 30 numbered sites for tents or RVs, for $8 per site, per night. Middle Lion Camp has six tent sites; an Adventure Pass (fee) is required for a parked vehicle. No sites are reservable or have hookups. Each site takes up to eight people. Lion Camp has blacktop camp roads and spurs. Middle Lion has dirt roads and grounds.

At Lion Camp, each site has a picnic table and a pedestal barbecue or a steel fire ring (with grill) or both. Vault toilets are provided at several locations and at the trailhead near the entrance. The camp has an information board and trash cans but no water.

At Middle Lion Camp, each site has a picnic table. Two sites each have a pedestal barbecue, and two other sites each have a pedestal barbecue and a steel fire ring (with grill). The camp has one vault toilet and trash receptacles but no water.

Note: both camps have been temporarily closed for the protection of endangered species, but are usually open otherwise from

April 1 to January 30. Camping limit is 14 days. The camps' sites are not reservable. Maximum RV length is 16 feet. Confine fires to the camps' barbecues and fire rings. Dogs must be leashed.

DIRECTIONS From Ojai, take State Highway 33 north about 14.5 miles to Rose Valley Road (Forest Road 6N31). Turn right (east). Go about 3 miles, and the road bends north. Go about 2 miles to Forest Road 22W06. Turn right (south) and go about half a mile to Middle Lion Camp at the road's end (sign says *Middle Lions*). Continue on Rose Valley Road, beyond Forest Road 22W06, about a mile to the road's end and Lion Camp (sign says *Lions*).

Piedra Blanca Corrals Group Camp
U.S. Forest Service

GENERAL SETTING (LOCATION, FEATURES, SUPPLIES IN-FORMATION) This primitive, equestrian group camp is located northeast of Wheeler Springs, in the Sespe Creek Valley within the Rose Valley Recreation Area. The elevation is 3100 feet. The camp is set next to Rose Valley Road, and both sit on a slightly inclined shelf. The camp is less than half a mile west of Lion Camp. Across the road, Lion Canyon Camp can be seen in the valley roughly 25 feet below. *Piedra Blanca* means *white stone* or *white rock*, in Spanish, and may refer to the white, angular, sandstone formations that can be seen to the northeast. Grayish green pines afford partial shade. Chaparral covers the hill next to camp.

Two horse corrals, a water trough, a hitching post, and a one-room brick shed for a horse are featured. *Corrals* is sometimes included in the camp's name partly to help identify the camp as an equestrian group camp and to distinguish it from another Piedra Blanca Camp, a wilderness hike-in camp, a few miles north.

One private, shaded site sits on a brick-reinforced embankment. For local hiking trails, see Lion Campground in this book.

Supplies are available in Ojai, 20 miles south. For more information, contact Los Padres National Forest's Ojai Ranger District.

SITES, FEES, FACILITIES, RESTRICTIONS This group camp consists of four nonreservable sites for tents or RVs (no hookups). The camp takes up to 50 people and has a dirt parking area. A parked vehicle requires an Adventure Pass (fee).

Each of the four sites has a picnic table and a steel fire ring with grill. A service table and a large brick barbecue are centrally

located. This group camp has a vault toilet and trash cans but no water or hookups.
Note: the camp has been temporarily closed for the protection of endangered species, but is usually open otherwise.
Camping limit is 14 days. Maximum RV length is 16 feet. Fires are permitted only in the camp's fire rings. Dogs must be leashed.

DIRECTIONS From Ojai, take State Highway 33 north about 14.5 miles to Rose Valley Road (Forest Road 6N31). Turn right (east). Go 3 miles, and the road bends north. Go about 2.7 miles to the camp on the road's right side (sign says *Piedra Blanca*).

Beaver Campground
U.S. Forest Service

GENERAL SETTING (LOCATION, FEATURES, SUPPLIES IN-FORMATION) This camp is located north of Wheeler Springs at an elevation of 3000 feet. Pine Mountain dominates the northern skyline. The short road to camp drops down below the highway into a wide canyon, the size of a small valley, through which Sespe Creek flows. Fishing is permitted (license required). Sites are set among the chaparral and have some privacy but little shade. For hikers, Middle Sespe Trail (22W04) leads eastward from camp and goes along the southern edge of the Sespe Wilderness.
Supplies are available in Ojai. For more information, contact the Ojai Ranger District of the Los Padres National Forest.

SITES, FEES, FACILITIES, RESTRICTIONS There are 12 non-reservable sites for tents or RVs, with blacktop or dirt-and-gravel spurs (no hookups). A parked vehicle requires an Adventure Pass.
Each site has a picnic table and a pedestal barbecue or a steel fire ring (without grill) or both. One large family site has two tables, two pedestal barbecues, and a steel fire ring (without grill). The camp has two vault toilets and a few trash cans but no water.
Note: the campground, creek, and some trails have been temporarily closed for the protection of endangered species, but are usually open otherwise (except during fires, etc.). Camping limit is 14 days. Maximum RV length is 23 feet. Fires are restricted to the camp's barbecues and fire rings. Dogs must be leashed.

DIRECTIONS From Ojai, take State Highway 33 north about 17 miles to a short side road (about 2.5 miles north of Rose Valley Road). Turn right (east) and go to the road's end and the camp.

VENTURA COUNTY MOUNTAIN AREA

LOCKWOOD VALLEY
AND
ADJACENT CAMPGROUNDS

▲8 Pine Mountain
▲9 Reyes Peak
▲10 Rancho Nuevo
▲11 Tinta
▲12 Ozena

▲13 Reyes Creek
▲14 Dome Springs
▲15 Pine Springs
▲16 Thorn Meadows
▲17 Half Moon

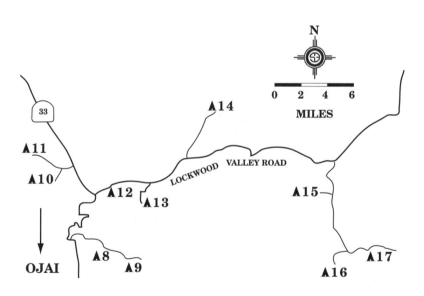

Pine Mountain Campground
Reyes Peak Campground
U.S. Forest Service

GENERAL SETTING (LOCATION, FEATURES, SUPPLIES, IN-FORMATION) High-altitude views of the Sespe Creek area to the south, from along the road which leads to these campgrounds, are breathtaking. On clear days, the Channel Islands and Pacific Ocean are visible to the southwest, from certain points along the road. These small, primitive tent camps are located near Reyes Peak, on Pine Mountain, north of Wheeler Springs. Camp elevations are over 6500 feet. *Reyes* is the Spanish word for *kings*.

Pine Mountain Campground is situated among tall pines in a bowl-shaped depression beside and slightly below the road. Along the road, about halfway between the two camps, is a horse corral and one picnic site with a picnic table and fire ring with grill.

Reyes Peak Campground sits at the edge of a cliff, with views, through the pines, of the Sespe Creek area to the south. About half the sites are farther down the road, away from the main part of camp, and are set among boulders. Near the entrance, a sign points you to Raspberry Spring, down the hill via a hiking trail. Phone for information on Raspberry Camp, a little hike-in camp.

Reyes Peak (7510 feet) is roughly 2 miles east of Reyes Peak Camp. The trailhead of the trail that leads up to the peak is reached at the end of Reyes Peak Road. *Caution:* the 1.5-mile stretch of dirt road from Reyes Peak Camp to the road's end is very poor, rocky and bumpy; four-wheel-drive vehicles are recommended.

Purchase supplies in Ojai before making the 30-mile trip to camp. For more information, write or phone the Ojai Ranger District of the Los Padres National Forest.

SITES, FEES, FACILITIES, RESTRICTIONS Each camp has six nonreservable, dirt tent sites (no developed spurs) with up to eight people per site. A parked vehicle requires an Adventure Pass.

Each campsite, at both camps, has a picnic table and a steel fire ring with grill. Each camp has a vault toilet, but no water.

Both camps are open from April to October (except during fires, rains, snows, etc.). *Caution:* the road to these camps is narrow, poorly paved with potholes, and has some stretches of dirt.

Camping limit is 14 days. Fires are permitted only in the camps' fire rings. Dogs must be leashed.

DIRECTIONS From Ojai, take State Highway 33 north about 31.5 miles to Reyes Peak Road (Forest Road 6N06), which has potholes. Turn right (east) and go about 4.5 miles to Pine Mountain Camp, then a mile to Reyes Peak Camp. Both camps are on the road's south side.

Rancho Nuevo Campground
Tinta Campground
U.S. Forest Service

GENERAL SETTING (LOCATION, FEATURES, SUPPLIES, INFORMATION) Wooded areas of pinyon pines form the settings of these tiny, primitive tent camps, located north of Ozena Forest Station, at an elevation over 3500 feet. The weather is pleasant during spring and fall, but fairly hot in the summer. Rancho Nuevo Camp and Tinta Camp were named for their respective creeks.

Rancho Nuevo Camp is set in a gorge, carved by Rancho Nuevo Creek. Steep stone cliffs with pines produce a picture that somewhat resembles many a canyon in the Rocky Mountains. Rancho Nuevo Trail (24W03) follows Rancho Nuevo Creek west from camp into the Dick Smith Wilderness. This trail reaches Deal Canyon Trail and Deal Junction about two miles west of camp. Phone for information on wilderness hike-in camps and regulations.

Tinta Camp sits in a deep, chaparral canyon surrounded by hills covered with pines and cedars. Tinta Creek Trail is an ORV trail designated for motorcycles. They may be operated only on roads and designated trails. The trail leads northwest from camp.

Halfway Station, with a restaurant and a rest area (not run by Caltrans), is on the west side of Highway 33, just north of Forest Road 7N04. Purchase supplies in Ojai, before driving the long distance to camp. For more information, write or phone the Mount Pinos Ranger District of the Los Padres National Forest.

SITES, FEES, FACILITIES, RESTRICTIONS Each camp has three nonreservable, dirt tent sites (no developed spurs), with up to eight people per site. A parked vehicle needs an Adventure Pass.

At Rancho Nuevo Camp, each site has a steel fire ring (with grill), and two campsites each have a picnic table, but there is no toilet. At Tinta Camp, each campsite has a picnic table and a steel fire ring (with grill), and the camp has a vault toilet. Neither camp has water or hookups. RVs must be self-contained.

Caution: the camps are open from late spring to early fall, but are subject to closure during rains. The dirt road to both camps is crossed by the Cuyama River, and the road to Tinta Camp is crossed by streams. The road to Rancho Nuevo Camp is periodically washed out. Four-wheel-drive vehicles are advised. Camping limit is 14 days. For fires, use only the camps' fire rings. Dogs must be leashed.

DIRECTIONS From Ojai, take State Highway 33 about 39.5 miles north to unpaved Forest Road 7N04 (about 2 miles north of Lockwood Valley Road). Turn left (west) and go about 0.75 mile to Forest Road 7N04A. Turn left (south) and go about 0.75 mile to Rancho Nuevo Camp. To reach Tinta Camp, stay on Forest Road 7N04, as it bends northwest, and go 2 miles to the road's end and the camp.

Ozena Campground
U.S. Forest Service

GENERAL SETTING (LOCATION, FEATURES, SUPPLIES, INFORMATION) Ozena Valley is a beautiful country area—quiet and hardly touched by civilization. Views of distant, pine-covered hills and of the oak valley add to the uplifting feeling here. Scattered rural ranches characterize the valley, nearly midway between Wheeler Springs and Ventucopa, in northern Ventura County. Campground elevation is 3660 feet. Fall and spring weather here is relatively mild for camping, whereas winters bring rain, and summers bring heat that increases forest fire danger.

Ozena Campground is a shaded spot near the highway and has two small, primitive camping areas, one on either side of Forest Road 9N03. Most campsites are shaded by oaks or cottonwoods, although one site on the west side is off by itself, in the brush, away from the trees. Tables at some campsites are partially buried by dirt and silt that settled and piled up from rain puddles. Some of the trees have unusual, twisted patterns on their bark.

The trailhead of Ozena Trail (23W42) is found near Ozena Fire Station and Highway 33. This steep, lengthy trail leads south, up Pine Mountain. Trail 24W04 can be found on the west side of Highway 33, about a mile south of Lockwood Valley Road. This steep, uphill trail leads west, through Bear Canyon, into the Dick Smith Wilderness. Phone for wilderness regulations.

Ozena Fire and Forest Stations are on the east side of Highway 33, just south of Lockwood Valley Road. Camp Scheideck village and Reyes Creek Camp are about 5 miles southeast of Ozena

Camp. There's not much else in the Ozena Valley. The Ozena and Scheideck post offices were open in the early 1900s and later closed. Limited supplies are available at Camp Scheideck Lodge in Camp Scheideck village, about 5 miles southeast (see Reyes Creek Campground). You can also stock up on supplies in Ojai, before driving north to Ozena Camp, since it is about a 40-mile drive on a winding canyon road. For more information, write or phone the Mount Pinos Ranger District of the Los Padres National Forest.

SITES, FEES, FACILITIES, RESTRICTIONS There are 10 non-reservable sites, 5 on each side of camp, for tents or RVs (no hookups). Up to eight people are allowed per site. A parked vehicle requires an Adventure Pass (fee). The camp has dirt sites.

Each site has a picnic table and a steel fire ring with grill. On each side of camp there are two vault toilets. There is no water. RV water and dump stations are at Tejon Pass Rest Area, on I-5, north of Frazier Park (about 34 miles northeast of camp).

The camp is open all year (except during fires, floods, etc.). Camping limit is 14 days. Maximum RV length is 22 feet. Fires are restricted to the camp's fire rings. Dogs must be leashed.

DIRECTIONS From Ojai, take State Highway 33 north about 37.5 miles to Lockwood Valley Road. Turn right (east) and go about 1.5 miles to Forest Road 9N03. Turn right, and go to the camp.

Reyes Creek Campground
U.S. Forest Service

GENERAL SETTING (LOCATION, FEATURES, SUPPLIES, INFORMATION) Camp Scheideck Lodge, established in the 1890s, and a small village of houses and cabins, add a quaint touch of civilization to this otherwise remote area. The campground is set in a wide place in a canyon of cottonwoods, oaks, a few small pines, and chaparral, and is located near the lodge. Reyes Creek flows through the canyon and by camp, hence the camp's name. Fishing is permitted at this creek (license required), and a fishing pier is provided with wheelchair access. The camp's elevation is 3960 feet.

For hikers or horseback riders, access to Piedra Blanca National Recreation Trail (22W03) can be found a quarter mile beyond Reyes Creek Campground. The trailhead is across the road from a large, paved parking area, with a vault toilet (wheelchair accessible) and a horse corral with a circular feeding trough. The trail follows Reyes Creek southeast through the Sespe Wilderness, for over 15 miles, and ends near Lion Campground. Phone for information on wilderness hike-in camps and regulations.

Supplies are available in Ojai. Limited groceries are available at Camp Scheideck Lodge. For more information, contact the Mount Pinos Ranger District of the Los Padres National Forest.

SITES, FEES, FACILITIES, RESTRICTIONS The camp has 29 individual, numbered sites, of which 23 are for tents, and 6 are for RVs or tents. The limit is eight people per individual site. There is also one group site. An Adventure Pass (fee) is required for each parked vehicle. The camp has paved camp roads and dirt sites.

Most individual sites each have a picnic table and a steel fire ring with grill. The camp has piped water spigots, vault toilets at the entrance and at the other side of camp, and two dumpsters at the entrance. There are no hookups. An RV water station and dump station are at Tejon Pass Rest Area, on I-5, north of Frazier Park (about 34 miles northeast of camp).

The group site, near the camp's entrance, has three picnic tables, a serving table, a steel fire ring with grill, and a small concrete barbecue. Water spigots and vault toilets are nearby.

The camp is usually open, but is subject to closure during rains or fires. *Caution:* Reyes Creek crosses Lockwood Valley Road, west of camp, and signs along this road alert you to flooding.

Camping limit is 14 days. No sites are reservable. Quiet hours are from 10 P.M. to 6 A.M. Maximum RV length is 22 feet. Confine fires to the camp's fire rings and barbecue. Dogs must be leashed.

DIRECTIONS From Ojai, take State Highway 33 north about 37.5 miles to Lockwood Valley Road. Turn right (east) and go about 3.5 miles to Forest Road 7N11 (Reyes Creek Road). Turn right (south) and go about 1.5 miles to the camp, just beyond Camp Scheideck Lodge. Drive through camp, and find the sign directing you to the trailhead for Piedra Blanca Trail (22W03). Follow the sign, and go about 0.2 mile to the trailhead and the parking area.

Dome Springs Campground
U.S. Forest Service

GENERAL SETTING (LOCATION, FEATURES, SUPPLIES, INFORMATION) This primitive, little tent camp is located in a wide place in East Dry Canyon, an area that approaches the size of a little valley. The camp sits at the southern edge of the Chumash Wilderness. Camp elevation is 4800 feet.

Campsites are spread out from each other. Short, scrub pines and other trees, along with lots of cedar bushes and chaparral, afford privacy at the campsites and partial shade. Some neighboring hills are covered by the same vegetation, while other hills are made of sandstone and are barren.

Supplies are available in Ojai and at Camp Scheideck Lodge, near Reyes Creek Campground. For more information, contact the Mount Pinos Ranger District of the Los Padres National Forest.

SITES, FEES, FACILITIES, RESTRICTIONS Four nonreservable dirt sites for tents (no developed spurs) take up to eight people per site. A parked vehicle requires an Adventure Pass (fee).

Each site has a picnic table. Each of three sites has a steel fire ring with grill. One site has a small concrete barbecue and a fire ring made of rocks and concrete (without grill). There is a centrally located vault toilet and an information board, but no water.

The camp is usually open, but is subject to closure during rains or fires. *Caution:* a sign says that only four-wheel-drive vehicles are allowed on the road to camp. This rough dirt road passes through a floodplain, is crossed in several places by streams, and wanders inside the streambed. Camping limit is 14 days. For fires, use only the camp's fire rings and barbecue. Dogs must be leashed.

DIRECTIONS From Ojai, take State Highway 33 north about 37.5 miles to Lockwood Valley Road. Turn right (east) and go about 6.5 miles to unpaved Forest Road 8N04 (dirt). Turn left (north) and go about 3 miles to the campground (camp sign missing).

Pine Springs Campground
U.S. Forest Service

GENERAL SETTING (LOCATION, FEATURES, SUPPLIES, INFORMATION) Pines decorate the local hills throughout the rural Lockwood Valley area and enhance the areas' beauty.

Though primitive, this camp is located in a small forested valley, on San Guillermo Creek bed, about halfway between Frazier Park and Ozena Forest Station. The camp is set on a slight slope of a hill, amid tall pines and sage. At the camp's elevation, 5800 feet, the summer heat is not as intense as elsewhere. Sites are well separated, shaded, and have some privacy.

Yellow Jacket Trail is for ORV use; phone for details. From Lockwood Valley Road, take Forest Road 7N03 south about 2 miles to unpaved Piano Box Loop Road, which loops around again to Forest Road 7N03, about half a mile farther south. Turn east on to Piano Box Loop Road, at either intersection, then go about 1.25 miles (as the signs say), and you will reach Yellow Jacket Trail.

Supplies are available in Frazier Park, northeast. Lake of the Woods has limited supplies. For more information, contact the Mount Pinos Ranger District of the Los Padres National Forest.

SITES, FEES, FACILITIES, RESTRICTIONS There are 12 non-reservable, numbered sites for tents or RVs (no hookups) with up to eight people per site. The camp has dirt sites and dirt parking spurs. An Adventure Pass (fee) is required for a parked vehicle.

Each site has a picnic table. Most sites each have a steel fire ring (with grill) or a small rock-and-concrete barbecue or both. Some sites each have a rock fire ring. There are two vault toilets and an information board (no water). Tejon Pass Rest Area, on I-5, north of Frazier Park, has RV water and dump stations.

The camp is open from May to October, but is subject to closure during rains or fires. *Caution:* portions of the roads leading to camp are unpaved (dirt) and are rough like washboard. Forest Road 7N03A is a rocky, bumpy, poor dirt road, recommended for four-wheel-drive vehicles but not trailers or motorhomes. Camping limit is 14 days. Maximum RV length is 22 feet. For fires, use only the camp's barbecues and fire rings. Dogs must be leashed.

DIRECTIONS From Ojai, take State Highway 33 north about 37.5 miles to Lockwood Valley Road. Turn right (east) and go about 16.5 miles to unpaved Forest Road 7N03. Turn right (south) and go about 2.5 miles to Forest Road 7N03A (dirt). Turn right (west) and go 0.75 mile to the road's end and the camp (sign missing).

Thorn Meadows Campground
U.S. Forest Service

GENERAL SETTING (LOCATION, FEATURES, SUPPLIES, INFORMATION) The Thorn Meadows area, in the remote woodlands, south of the Lockwood Valley, is the setting of this small, remote, primitive campground. The elevation at camp is 5000 feet.

The camp sits in a narrow canyon, on a bluff, roughly 20 feet high, which overlooks one of Piru Creek's forks. Though the camp's site is not a meadow in the usual sense, it is nevertheless scenic, with some Jeffrey pines and sandstone formations, such as the balanced rock, on the hill above the restroom, behind camp.

A horse corral, water trough, and an unwalled horse shed are provided, just north of camp, on the west side of Thorn Meadows Road. Across that road, between the corral and camp, is a parking area next to the old Thorn Meadows Guard Station which is closed at this writing. A trailhead is found about half a mile north of the corral, on Thorn Meadows Road. As the sign says, the trail is Cedar Creek Trail (21W06), and it leads west several miles into the Sespe Wilderness. Phone for information on wilderness hike-in camps in that area and for wilderness camping regulations.

Another horse corral can be found on Forest Road 7N03, about half a mile north of Thorn Meadows Road. Those who relish a steep, uphill hike, might consider Thorn Point Trail (21W07), which stretches from Thorn Meadows Campground southwest about 3 miles to Thorn Point Lookout (nearly 7000 feet in elevation).

Supplies are available in Ojai and Frazier Park. For more information, write or phone the Mount Pinos Ranger District of the Los Padres National Forest.

SITES, FEES, FACILITIES, RESTRICTIONS Three nonreservable dirt sites for tents (no developed spurs) take up to eight people per site. A parked vehicle requires an Adventure Pass (fee).

Two sites each have a picnic table and a steel fire ring with grill; one of these sites has two picnic tables. The site on the hill has a picnic table and a small concrete barbecue. The camp has two vault toilets, but no water or hookups. RV water and dump stations are at Tejon Pass Rest Area, on I-5, north of Frazier Park.

The camp is open from May to October, but subject to closure during rains or fires. *Caution:* the dirt roads are poor and crossed by Piru Creek and its forks, even in dry weather. Four-wheel-drive vehicles are strongly recommended for these stream crossings. The side road to camp is very poor, narrow, and crossed by streams.

Camping limit is 14 days. Maximum RV length is 16 feet. Fires are allowed only in the camp's fire rings and its barbecue. Dogs must be leashed.

DIRECTIONS From Ojai, take State Highway 33 north about 38 miles to Lockwood Valley Road. Turn right (east) and go 16.5 miles to unpaved Forest Road 7N03. Turn right (south) and go about 7.5 miles to a fork in the road. The sign there says THORN MEADOWS

CAMPGROUND 2 [miles] with an arrow pointing to the right (southwest). Bear to the right, on unpaved Thorn Meadows Road, and go about 2 miles to the road's end and the camp (camp sign missing).

Half Moon Campground
U.S. Forest Service

GENERAL SETTING (LOCATION, FEATURES, SUPPLIES, INFORMATION) The Piru Creek area, in the quiet woodlands, south of the Lockwood Valley, is the location of this remote, primitive campground. The camp is in a small, bowl-shaped valley, about a quarter mile wide, surrounded by pine-covered hills and some bare hills. Tall pines afford shade. The elevation is 4700 feet.

A lengthy hiking trail (20W12) leads southeast from Mutau Flat to Johnson Ridge. Stay on Forest Road 7N03, beyond the turnoff to camp, and go about 2 miles to the end of the road and the trailhead (follow the signs). The trail goes into the Sespe Wilderness. Phone for wilderness regulations.

Supplies are available in Ojai and Frazier Park. For more information, write or phone the Mount Pinos Ranger District of the Los Padres National Forest.

SITES, FEES, FACILITIES, RESTRICTIONS There are 10 nonreservable dirt sites for tents or RVs, with dirt spurs and up to eight people per site. A parked vehicle requires an Adventure Pass.

Each site has a picnic table and a steel fire ring with grill. The camp has two vault toilets, centrally located, but no water or hookups. An RV water station and dump station are located at Tejon Pass Rest Area, on I-5, north of Frazier Park.

The camp is open from May to October, but is subject to closure during rains or fires. *Caution:* the dirt access roads are poor and crossed in several places by Piru Creek. Four-wheel-drive vehicles are strongly recommended for these creek crossings.

Camping limit is 14 days. Maximum RV length is 22 feet. Fires are restricted to the camp's fire rings. Dogs must be leashed.

DIRECTIONS From Ojai, take State Highway 33 north about 37.5 miles to Lockwood Valley Road. Turn right (east) and go 16.5 miles to unpaved Forest Road 7N03. Turn right (south) and go about 10 miles to a sign that says FOREST ROAD 7N13. Turn left (north), and go 0.25 mile to the road's end and the camp (sign missing).

VENTURA COUNTY MOUNTAIN AREA

NORTHERN COUNTY AND ADJACENT CAMPGROUNDS

▲18 Nettle Springs
▲19 Ballinger
▲20 Valle Vista
▲21 Marian
▲22 Caballo
▲23 Toad Springs
▲24 Campo Alto

▲25 Mil Potrero Park
▲26 McGill
    McGill Group
▲27 Mount Pinos
▲28 Chula Vista
▲29 Chuchupate
    Tejon Pass Rest Area

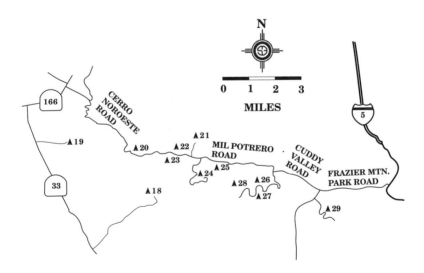

Nettle Springs Campground
U.S. Forest Service

GENERAL SETTING (LOCATION, FEATURES, SUPPLIES, IN-FORMATION) Named for a local spring, this primitive camp-ground is remotely located in Apache Canyon, on the western edge of the Chumash Wilderness, between Wheeler Springs and Ventucopa. The elevation at camp is 4400 feet. The camp is in a light-ly forested glen of pinyon pines, cedar bushes, and chaparral. Apache Canyon Creek divides the camp in half. Springs, west of camp, feed a water trough provided for horses and other livestock.

At the canyon entrance, pines are visible only on the hills above. Farther along the canyon, scattered, short, scrub pines, grayish green in color, gradually appear on the canyon floor. These even-tually yield to taller, dark green pines, closer to camp.

A short ORV trail is half a mile west of camp, via Apache Can-yon Road. Other short ORV trails can be found along Apache Can-yon Road, about 2 miles and 4.5 miles east of Highway 33. These ORV trails are for various kinds of ORV use.

Purchase supplies in Ojai or Frazier Park before making the long trip to camp. For more information, contact the Mount Pinos Ranger District of the Los Padres National Forest.

SITES, FEES, FACILITIES, RESTRICTIONS There are nine nonreservable dirt sites, of which four sites are for tents or RVs (no hookups). The rest are for tents only and are across the creek, south of the main part of camp. Up to eight people are allowed at each site. An Adventure Pass (fee) is required for a parked vehicle.

About half the sites each have a picnic table. Most sites each have a steel fire ring. The camp has two vault toilets but no water. There are RV water and dump stations at Tejon Pass Rest Area, on I-5, north of Frazier Park (about 35 miles east of Highway 33).

The camp is usually open, but is subject to closure during rains, floods, or fires. *Caution:* a sign says that only four-wheel-drive vehicles are allowed on Apache Canyon Road, a rutty dirt road of 8 miles in length that is crossed in several places by Apache Can-yon Creek. Camping limit is 14 days. Maximum RV length is 20 feet. For fires, use only the camp's fire rings. Dogs must be leashed.

DIRECTIONS From Ojai, take State Highway 33 north about 43 miles to unpaved Apache Canyon Road (Forest Road 8N06). Turn right (east) and go about 8.5 miles to camp (camp sign missing).

Ballinger Campground
U.S. Forest Service

GENERAL SETTING (LOCATION, FEATURES, SUPPLIES, IN-FORMATION) The Ballinger Canyon Off-Road Vehicle (ORV) Area, within the greater Ballinger-Deer Park ORV area, is the main reason for the popularity of this primitive camp, located in northwestern Ventura County. The campground sits in a bowl-shaped valley, about half a mile wide, within the badlands of Ballinger Canyon, at an elevation of 3000 feet. Sites are spread out and set among cedar bushes which give some privacy, but little shade. The camp has views of the angular, bare hills nearby. Spring and fall have the best weather, but summer can get very hot.

The Ballinger-Deer Park ORV area, developed with funds from California's Green Sticker program, contains about 7500 acres, and includes portions of Ballinger and Deer Park Canyons. Each ORV trail has a sign that indicates what kinds of ORVs may be used and the trail's degree of difficulty. An ORV information board, near the camp entrance, describes the ORV area, lists ORV rules, and displays maps of the ORV trails.

Per State regulations, "All vehicles must either be registered street-legal vehicles or have a State of California off-highway registration (Green Sticker)." ORVs must stay in areas and on trails designated for ORV use. An Adventure Pass is not required for ORV Green Sticker use; display your sticker. Please follow ORV rules, so that this activity may continue for everyone.

New Cuyama has limited supplies and gasoline, about 15 miles northwest on Highway 166. For more information, contact the Mount Pinos Ranger District of the Los Padres National Forest.

SITES, FEES, FACILITIES, RESTRICTIONS There are 20 non-reservable dirt sites for tents or RVs (no hookups), with up to eight people per site. The camp has dirt spurs and dirt roads. An Adventure Pass (fee) is required for each street-legal vehicle parked on national forest land.

Most sites each have a steel fire ring (with grill); one site has a pedestal barbecue. Most sites each have a picnic table. There are vault toilets at three locations (no water). Tejon Pass Rest Area, about 50 miles east, on I-5, has RV water and dump stations.

The camp is usually open, but is subject to closure during rains or fires. *Caution:* the paved road to camp is narrow and crossed by a stream, and therefore could be impassable in rainy weather.

Camping limit is 14 days. Maximum RV length is 32 feet. No fires are permitted except in the camp's fire rings and its barbecue. A permit is required for portable stoves. Dogs must be leashed.

DIRECTIONS From Ojai, take State Highway 33 north about 54 miles to Ballinger Canyon Road (Forest Road 9N10). Turn right (east) and go about 3 miles to camp, at the road's end.

Valle Vista Campground
U.S. Forest Service

GENERAL SETTING (LOCATION, FEATURES, SUPPLIES, INFORMATION) *Valle Vista* means *valley view*, a perfect name for this little camp with its stunning view of the San Joaquin Valley in the distance (on a clear day). One campsite sits at the edge of the hill and takes in this view. The camp is situated on a wide, level place on the side of a hill, below the highway, about 25 miles west of Frazier Park. Pinyon and oak trees partially shade the camp, at an elevation of 4800 feet. Fall and spring have mild weather, with fresh mountain air. Winters are rainy, and summers warm.

Supplies, gasoline, and phones are available in Pine Mountain Club, 11.5 miles east. For more information, contact the Mount Pinos Ranger District of the Los Padres National Forest.

SITES, FEES, FACILITIES, RESTRICTIONS There are seven nonreservable dirt sites for tents or RVs (no hookups) with up to eight people per site. A parked vehicle requires an Adventure Pass.

Each site has a steel fire ring with grill. Most sites each have a table. A short trail leads east to four vault toilets on a knoll. There is no water. Tejon Pass Rest Area, on I-5, north of Frazier Park has RV water and dump stations (28 miles east of camp).

This camp is usually open (except during fires, etc.). *Caution:* a short, somewhat steep, bumpy, dirt access road leads down from the highway to camp. For details, see Directions below.

Camping limit is 14 days. Maximum RV length is 32 feet. Fires are restricted to the camp's fire rings. Dogs must be leashed.

DIRECTIONS From I-5, take the Frazier Park exit (Frazier Mountain Park Road). Go west 7 miles. At the fork, in Lake of the Woods, bear right (northwest) on Cuddy Valley Road. Go about 5 miles to the next fork, and turn right at Mil Potrero Road (heading northwest). Go about 8 miles to Cerro Noroeste Road. Turn right (west) and go about 9.5 miles. *Caution:* the camp's steep, dirt access road meets the highway at such a sharp angle, that the turn north-ward into camp can only be made safely and easily from the east-bound direction, by most vehicles. Those going westbound on the highway will have to pass the camp, turn around, come back, and turn north into camp from the eastbound side of the highway.

Marian and Caballo Campgrounds
U.S. Forest Service

GENERAL SETTING (LOCATION, FEATURES, SUPPLIES, IN-FORMATION) Woodlands of Jeffrey pines and pinyon trees, west of Pine Mountain Club, form the settings of these small camps. The elevation is 6600 feet at Marian Camp, near the top of a ridge, and is 5800 feet at Caballo Camp, down in a canyon.

Marian Campground is primitive and not easily accessible, but sits in an attractive, bowl-shaped area just below the crest of Blue Ridge. Tall pines are scattered throughout camp, and a pine forest surrounds the camp. Enjoy the view, from the northern rim, of the valley below. San Emigdio Jeep Trail (107) is a designated off-road vehicle (ORV) trail open to jeeps, motorcycles, and ATVs.

Caballo Campground sits at a partly shaded clearing in a broad canyon bottom, on the way to Marian Camp. *Caballo* means *horse*, in Spanish, and is an appropriate name here, since horseback riding is one of the safest ways to get from Caballo Camp to Marian Camp. At times a camp host resides at Caballo Camp.

Supplies and gasoline are available in Pine Mountain Club and Frazier Park to the east. For more information, contact the Mount Pinos Ranger District of the Los Padres National Forest.

SITES, FEES, FACILITIES, RESTRICTIONS Each camp has five nonreservable dirt sites for tents or RVs, with up to eight persons per site. A parked vehicle requires an Adventure Pass.

At Marian Camp, each site has a picnic table and a steel fire ring (with grill). At Caballo Camp, each site has a picnic table and a steel fire ring (with grill) or a small concrete barbecue. Caballo Camp has vault toilets, but Marian Camp does not (as of this writing). Neither camp has piped water or hookups. RV water and dump stations are provided at Tejon Pass Rest Area, on I-5, north of Frazier Park (about 22 miles east of Forest Road 9N27).

Extreme caution is advised on the very narrow (one lane), steep, dirt road between Caballo Camp and Marian Camp. The wheel track is about 2 feet from the edge, with a steep drop-off of over

100 feet on one side, and there are no turnouts. The portion of this dirt road from the highway to Caballo Camp is somewhat better. The camps are open from May to November (closed during fires). Camping limit is 14 days. Maximum RV length is 16 feet. For fires, use only the camps' barbecues and fire rings. Dogs must be leashed.

DIRECTIONS From I-5, take the Frazier Park exit (Frazier Mountain Park Road). Go west about 7 miles. At the fork, in Lake of the Woods, bear right (northwest) on Cuddy Valley Road. Go about 5 miles to the next fork, and turn right at Mil Potrero Road (heading northwest). Go about 8 miles to Cerro Noroeste Road. Turn right (west) and go about 1.2 mile to unpaved Forest Road 9N27. Turn right (north) and go half a mile to Caballo Camp (camp sign missing). Go about 1.5 miles to the road's end and Marian Camp.

Toad Springs Campground
U.S. Forest Service

GENERAL SETTING (LOCATION, FEATURES, SUPPLIES, INFORMATION) This primitive little camp, west of Pine Mountain Club, is near the main highway, but appears very rustic, as if far from civilization. The camp is set in an open clearing, near a creek and spring, at the shallow eastern end of Quatal Canyon. A few trees provided some shade. The elevation is 5700 feet.

For hikers, Toad Springs Trail (22W01) leads southwest from Toad Springs Campground to Mesa Springs Trail (22W21), in the Chumash Wilderness. Phone for wilderness regulations.

Supplies and gasoline are available in Pine Mountain Club and Frazier Park to the east. For more information, contact the Mount Pinos Ranger District of the Los Padres National Forest.

SITES, FEES, FACILITIES, RESTRICTIONS Six nonreservable dirt tent sites are for up to eight people per site. Four of these sites have short dirt spurs for RVs. A small parking area is at the rear of camp. A parked vehicle requires an Adventure Pass (fee).

Each campsite a steel fire ring (with grill) or a small concrete barbecue. Half the sites each have a picnic table. Some sites are shaded. The camp has no toilet, water, or hookups. An RV water station and dump station are available at Tejon Pass Rest Area, on I-5, north of Frazier Park (about 22 miles east of camp).

The camp is open from May to November. *Caution:* the short, dirt access road is poorly graded, crossed by a stream, and not recommended for large trailers and motorhomes. Camping limit is 14 days. Maximum RV length is 16 feet. Fires are restricted to the camp's barbecues and fire rings. Dogs must be leashed.

DIRECTIONS From I-5, take the Frazier Park exit (Frazier Mountain Park Road). Go west about 7 miles. At the fork, in Lake of the Woods, bear right (northwest) on Cuddy Valley Road. Go about 5 miles to the next fork, and turn right at Mil Potrero Road (heading northwest). Go about 8 miles to Cerro Noroeste Road. Turn right (west) and go a mile to rough Quatal Canyon Road (dirt). Turn left and go a quarter mile to camp (camp sign missing).

Campo Alto Campground
U.S. Forest Service

GENERAL SETTING (LOCATION, FEATURES, SUPPLIES, INFORMATION) This camp is located on Cerro Noroeste (Mount Abel), at an elevation of 8250 feet. Most sites are shaded, and from some parts of camp there are views through the trees of the valley below. Also enjoy spectacular views of the Cuyama Valley (to the west) and of the distant, desert-like Carrizo Plain (northwest), while driving along Cerro Noroeste Road, on the way to camp.

Mount Pinos Trail (21W03) is a hiking trail of about 4.5 miles leading southeast, through the woodlands of the Mount Pinos Recreation Area, to Mount Pinos. Caution is advised due to the steepness of the trail and the elevation of the area. This trail is better suited to experienced hikers who are physically fit. The trailhead is on the main road, about 0.7 mile before reaching camp.

Supplies, gasoline, and phones are available in Pine Mountain Club to the east. For more information, write or phone the Mount Pinos Ranger District of the Los Padres National Forest.

SITES, FEES, FACILITIES, RESTRICTIONS The camp has 15 individual, numbered dirt sites for tents or RVs (no hookups). Up to eight people are allowed at each individual site. An Adventure Pass (fee) is required for a parked vehicle.

Each individual site has a picnic table and a steel fire ring (with grill) or a small concrete barbecue. Vault toilets are located near the camp's entrance and at the rear of camp.

Two group sites are at the rear of camp. One has five picnic tables, the other has a long picnic table, and both sites each have a large, waist-high, concrete barbecue. Vault toilets are nearby.

No sites are reservable. The camp has no water (bring your own). RV water and dump stations are located at Tejon Pass Rest Area, on I-5, north of Frazier Park (28 miles northeast of camp). This camp is open from May to November (closed during fires). Camping limit is 14 days. Maximum RV length is 22 feet. For fires, use only the camp's barbecues and fire rings. Dogs must be leashed.

DIRECTIONS From I-5, take the Frazier Park exit (Frazier Mountain Park Road). Go west about 7 miles. At the fork, in Lake of the Woods, bear right (northwest) on Cuddy Valley Road. Go about 5 miles to the next fork, and turn right at Mil Potrero Road (heading northwest). Go about 8 miles to Cerro Noroeste Road (Forest Road 9N07). Turn left (south), and go about 7.7 miles to the camp at the road's end, just beyond the old lodge (camp sign missing).

Mil Potrero Park

GENERAL SETTING (LOCATION, FEATURES, SUPPLIES, INFORMATION) This rustic park with campground, located west of the village of Pine Mountain Club, is on property leased from the U.S. Forest Service to West Side Recreation and Park District in Taft. The campground is situated in a small, inviting valley of scattered pines, near the highway, at an elevation of 5000 feet.

The park features a playground near the picnic area, a recreation hall, a volleyball court, horseshoe pits, and horse corrals.

Supplies, gasoline, and phones are available in Pine Mountain Club, about 1.5 miles east of Mil Potrero Park. For more information, write or phone West Side Recreation and Park District.

SITES, FEES, FACILITIES, RESTRICTIONS There are 34 sites in the RV section (no hookups), and 9 sites in the tent section. The nightly fee for district residents is $10 per site, and for all others it is $15 per site. Some sites are wheelchair accessible.

Most sites each have a picnic table and a pedestal barbecue or a steel fire ring (with grill); some tent sites have a fire pit. Some large family sites have two picnic tables and both a fire ring and a barbecue. Every site has a trash can. RV sites have gravel spurs.

The RV and tent areas each have water spigots and a restroom with sinks, showers (for camping visitors only), and flush toilets. An RV dump station is available at Tejon Pass Rest Area, on I-5, north of Frazier Park (about 20 miles east of the park).

A four-bedroom, furnished cabin is available for $50 nightly for district residents, and $65 nightly for nondistrict residents. A cleaning and security deposit of $100 is also required. Mil Potrero Lodge has six large tables and over 30 chairs. The maximum dining capacity is 72, and the maximum assembly capacity is 150. Phone for lodge party fees, reservations, and rules.

The day-use picnic area has picnic tables and a restroom with sinks and flush toilets, but no fire rings or barbecues. Day-use fees are $3 per car, $5 per van, $10 per bus. The use of horse corrals is for temporary stabling only, and requires no fee for registered campers or registered day-use visitors.

The park is usually open (closed during fires, snows, etc.). Camping limit is 14 days. Quiet hours are from 10 P.M. to 7 A.M. No more than 10 people and 2 vehicles, including an RV, are allowed at each campsite. Maximum RV length is 28 feet. All vehicles must be street legal. Motorcycles may only be ridden from the campsite straight out of the park and back to the campsite.

Charcoal cooking fires are permitted only in the park's barbecues or in portable barbecues. Signs warn of high fire danger. Wood campfires are permitted only in the park's fire rings, and no paper or garbage may be burned. Fires must not exceed 3 feet in height. Only down wood may be gathered; firewood is sold in Pine Mountain Club. Dogs must be leashed (limit two dogs per site). Owners must clean up after their pets. A sign says BEWARE OF BEARS.

DIRECTIONS From I-5, take the Frazier Park exit (Frazier Mountain Park Road). Go west about 7 miles. At the fork, in Lake of the Woods, bear right (northwest) on Cuddy Valley Road. Go about 5 miles to the next fork, and turn right at Mil Potrero Road (heading northwest). Go about 7 miles to the park entrance, on the left (south) side of the road.

McGill Campground
McGill Group Camp
U.S. Forest Service

GENERAL SETTING (LOCATION, FEATURES, SUPPLIES, INFORMATION) These mountain camps sit amid towering Jeffrey pines at an elevation of 7400 feet. They are located together, about 5 miles east of Mount Pinos summit, and are within the Mount Pinos Recreation Area. At times a camp host resides in camp. The camps were placed on the inner side of the road, on the gentle slope of the hill, rather than on the road's outer side, at the edge of the cliff. This, with the pines, brings a feeling of privacy.

The Exploration Trail (a nature trail) is just beyond McGill Group Camp. The trail is a quarter mile long (a half mile for a round trip). It is a paved trail, accessible to wheel chairs. No horses, bikes, or all-terrain vehicles are allowed. Across from the trailhead are two wheelchair-accessible toilets next to a few wheelchair-access parking spaces. For a lengthy hike, McGill Trail takes you from camp several miles down to Cuddy Valley Road, about half a mile south of where it joins Mil Potrero Road.

Supplies and gas are available in Pine Mountain Club, and limited supplies in Lake of the Woods. For more information, phone the concessionaire, or contact the Mount Pinos Ranger District of the Los Padres National Forest.

SITES, FEES, FACILITIES, RESTRICTIONS There are 78 individual, nonreservable, numbered sites for tents or RVs. The nightly fee of $8 per site includes one vehicle and up to eight people. The fee is $5 for an additional vehicle. The camp has some blacktop spurs and blacktop roads. The day-use fee is $4 per vehicle.

Each individual site has a picnic table and a steel fire ring (with grill) or a small concrete barbecue. There are water spigots and vault toilets at several locations in camp, but no hookups.

There are two reservable group sites. One site takes a limit of 60 people, and the other site takes a limit of 80 people. The fee is $75 per site, per night. The reservation fee is $8.65 per group site.

Each group site has several picnic tables, small concrete barbecues, water spigots, vault toilets, a group parking area, and a rock fire ring with benches around it, like a campfire circle.

A dumpster is located near the main entrance. Firewood is for sale in camp when the camp host is present. An RV dump station is provided at Tejon Pass Rest Area, on I-5, north of Frazier Park (about 17 miles northeast of the camps).

The camps are open from June to October (closed during fires, heavy rains, etc.). Camping limit is 14 days. Quiet time is from 10 P.M. to 10 A.M. Maximum RV length is 16 feet. Fires are permitted only in the camps' barbecues and fire rings. Dogs must be leashed.

DIRECTIONS From I-5, take the Frazier Park exit (Frazier Mountain Park Road). Go west about 7 miles. At the fork, in Lake of the Woods, bear right (northwest) on Cuddy Valley Road (to Mount Pinos). Go about 5 miles to the next fork, and bear left (south) on Cuddy Valley Road (to Mount Pinos). After about half a mile, pass the trailhead of McGill Trail on the right side (for a hike of several miles up to McGill Camp). Continue on the road, about 4.5 miles, and turn right at the McGill Campground entrance road, which accesses the individual sites and group sites.

Mount Pinos Campground
U.S. Forest Service

GENERAL SETTING (LOCATION, FEATURES, SUPPLIES, INFORMATION) This campground commands views of the Lockwood Valley to the southeast and Frazier Mountain to the east. The camp is shaded by Jeffrey pines, at an elevation of 7800 feet, and is within the Mount Pinos Recreation Area. Mount Pinos summit is several miles west of camp. Mount Pinos was well named, as *pinos* is a Spanish word meaning *pines*, and pines certainly define this and many other mountain regions. For information on Mount Pinos area hiking, see Chula Vista Campground (below).

Supplies are available in Pine Mountain Club. For more information, phone the concessionaire, or contact the Mount Pinos Ranger District of the Los Padres National Forest.

SITES, FEES, FACILITIES, RESTRICTIONS This camp has 19 nonreservable sites for tents or RVs (no hookups), for $10 per site, per night. Up to eight persons are allowed at each site.

Each site has a picnic table and has a steel fire ring (with grill), or a rock fire pit, or both. The camp has piped water spigots, four vault toilets, and a dumpster. Water is limited, so as a precaution, bring your own. A parking area, suitable for day-use visitors, is along the main road, at the camp entrance. RV water and dump stations are provided at Tejon Pass Rest Area, on I-5, north of Frazier Park (about 19 miles northeast of camp).

The camp is open from June to October (closed during fires, heavy rains, etc.). Camping limit is 14 days. Maximum RV length is 16 feet. Quiet hours are from 10 P.M. to 10 A.M. Fires are restricted to the camp's fire rings and fire pits. Dogs must be leashed.

DIRECTIONS Use directions for McGill Campground, but stay on Cuddy Valley Road, and go beyond McGill Campground about 1.5 miles farther to Mount Pinos Campground.

Chula Vista Campground
U.S. Forest Service

GENERAL SETTING (LOCATION, FEATURES, SUPPLIES, INFORMATION) The large, paved, trailhead parking area at the end of Cuddy Valley Road serves hikers using the various trails in the central Mount Pinos Recreation Area, including the short trail (of 500 feet) on which to walk to Chula Vista Camp. This tent camp and picnic area is a quiet, secluded spot in the middle of a dense and shady Jeffrey pine forest on somewhat rolling terrain.

The sign on the small wooden building, near the trail to camp, says MOUNT PINOS NORDIC BASE and ELEVATION 8300 FEET. A sign on the building's front wall says FIRST AID CENTER FOR SOUTHERN CALIFORNIA NORDIC SKI PATROL.

Mount Pinos summit (elevation: 8831 feet) is about 2 miles west of this campground, reached by a dirt road at the front of the parking area. This road is for hikers and is gated to keep out vehicles. From the summit, Mount Pinos Trail (21W03) leads about 4.5 miles northwest to Cerro Noroeste Road, which in turn leads to the right to Campo Alto Campground, about 0.7 mile away, at the end of Cerro Noroeste Road. Caution is advised due to the steepness of the trail and the elevation of the area. This trail is better suited to experienced, physically fit hikers.

Supplies and gas are available in Pine Mountain Club and Lake of the Woods (limited). For more information, contact the Mount Pinos Ranger District of the Los Padres National Forest.

SITES, FEES, FACILITIES, RESTRICTIONS This camp has 10 nonreservable, walk-in dirt sites for tents only. Some sites are numbered, but numbers are missing at other sites. No more than eight persons are allowed at each site. An Adventure Pass (fee) is required for a vehicle parked in the trailhead parking area, whether for overnight camping or for day-use picnicking.

Each site has a picnic table; one site has two picnic tables. Each site has a steel fire ring (with grill), or a small concrete barbecue, or a rock fire pit. Some sites each have a fire ring and a barbecue. The campground has four vault toilets, but no water.

The camp is open from June to October. *Caution:* road signs warn that this is an area of extreme fire danger. Camping limit is 14 days. No fires are permitted except in the camp's barbecues, fire rings, and fire pits. Dogs must be leashed.

DIRECTIONS Use directions for McGill Campground, but stay on Cuddy Valley Road, and go beyond McGill Campground about 3.5 miles farther to the end of the road and the large parking area.

As you enter this parking area, you are facing north. To the left (west) of where you enter is the turnoff to the gated 2-mile road to Mount Pinos, on which hiking is permitted (no vehicles). Just beyond that turnoff, in the parking area, are portable toilets. At the rear of the parking lot (north side) is the little wooden building, "Mount Pinos Nordic Base." To the right (east) of the building, at the northwest corner of the parking area, is the entrance to the trail leading north to Chula Vista Campground. A short way down the trail, you reach a fork. At this fork, bear to the *right*, taking the right-hand (easternmost) trail, then go about 500 feet to camp. The trail goes along the east side of the meadow.

Back at the fork, the left (westernmost) trail leads a short way west to the dirt hiking road, which in turn leads about 2 miles to Mount Pinos summit. *Note:* the trail signs are somewhat unclear.

Chuchupate Campground
U.S. Forest Service

GENERAL SETTING (LOCATION, FEATURES, SUPPLIES, INFORMATION) This temporarily closed camp is southwest of Frazier Park, near the gateway to the Lockwood Valley. Hills thickly covered with pines can be seen surrounding the valley. The campground sits in a glade on the side of Frazier Mountain, at an elevation of 6200 feet. Sites are placed among stands of tall pines and cedars that provide shade. Frazier Mountain Lookout is roughly 4 miles farther east, but the road is dirt and very poor. Four-wheel-drive vehicles are recommended on that stretch. Chuchupate Ranger Station is 3 miles west of camp on Forest Road 8N04.

Supplies are available in Frazier Park and Lake of the Woods. For more information, write or phone the Mount Pinos Ranger District of the Los Padres National Forest.

SITES, FEES, FACILITIES, RESTRICTIONS There are 24 non-reservable dirt sites for tents or RVs (no hookups). Up to eight persons are allowed at each site. A parked vehicle requires an Adventure Pass (fee).

Each campsite has a picnic table and a steel fire ring with grill. The camp has vault toilets and an information board, but no water or hookups. RVs must be self-contained. RV water and dump stations are available at Tejon Pass Rest Area, on I-5, north of Frazier Park (about 12 miles northeast of camp).

Note: the campground has been temporarily closed. The camp is open otherwise from April to October (except during fires, etc.). *Caution:* the road that leads up Frazier Mountain to camp has deep potholes. This road is narrow and winding, with a steep drop-off, and there is danger of coming too close to its edge.

Camping limit is 14 days. Maximum RV length is 20 feet. Fires are allowed only in the camp's fire rings. Dogs must be leashed.

DIRECTIONS From I-5, take the Frazier Park exit (Frazier Mountain Park Road). Go west about 7 miles. At the fork, in Lake of the Woods, bear left (south), continuing on Frazier Mountain Park Road about a mile. At Forest Road 8N04, turn left (east). Go about 2.7 miles to the campground on the left (camp sign missing).

Tejon Pass Rest Area

Sycamore trees and lawns make this CALTRANS rest area a pleasant place to stop and stretch, nearly midway between Valencia and Bakersfield. It is located next to I-5 in a canyon near Frazier Park in Kern County. No camping is permitted. A travel stop with restaurants and gas stations is nearby at Frazier Park Junction, where Frazier Mountain Park Road meets the I-5 freeway. Another travel stop is found at Gorman, just 3.5 miles south. *Tejon* is the Spanish word for *badger*, a local woodland critter. Fort Tejon State Historic Park is about 4 miles north, via I-5.

This rest area is better equipped than most others. Its RV dump station serves several mountain campgrounds in the three-county border area (Los Angeles, Ventura, and Kern counties). Near the dump station is a water station with potable water to fill RV tanks. Picnic tables, picnic shelters (ramadas), benches, and drinking fountains are available. Vending machines dispense soft drinks, chips, candy, ice cream, etc. Other facilities include pay phones, newspaper vending machines, information boards, trash cans, and recycling bins. Restrooms have sinks and flush toilets and are wheelchair accessible, as are the paved pathways throughout the rest area. Dogs must be leashed. A pet area is provided.

From Valencia, take I-5 north about 35 miles. The rest area exit is just north of the Frazier Park exit, and south of the Lebec exit. State Highway 138, which leads east to Lancaster, Palmdale, and the Mojave Desert, is about 6 miles south of the rest area.

VENTURA COUNTY MOUNTAIN AREA

HUNGRY VALLEY SVRA
AND
ADJACENT CAMPGROUNDS

▲30 Hungry Valley SVRA
▲30A Edison
▲30B Sterling Canyon
▲30C Circle Canyon
▲30D Cottonwood
▲30E Upper Scrub Oaks
▲30F Lower Scrub Oaks
▲30G Smith Forks
▲30H Aliklik
▲30I Lane Ranch

▲31 Kings
▲32 Gold Hill
▲33 Dutchman
▲34 Twin Pines
▲35 Los Alamos
      Los Alamos
        Group
▲36 Hardluck

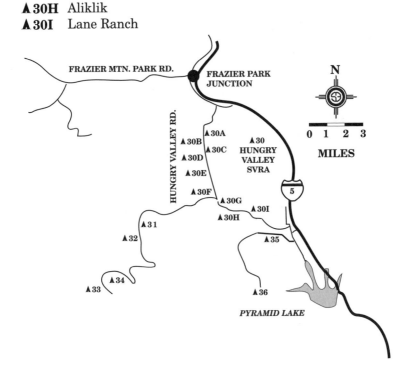

Hungry Valley State Vehicular Recreation Area (SVRA)

GENERAL SETTING (LOCATION, FEATURES, SUPPLIES, INFORMATION) This 19,000-acre SVRA is located south of Gorman. Registered vehicles such as motorcycles, four-wheel-drive vehicles, all-terrain vehicles (ATVs), and other off-highway vehicles (OHVs) can be driven on over 100 miles of OHV trails in this SVRA. In spring, wildflower tours are given; phone for information.

Special OHV features, on the west side of the SVRA, include a mini-track for beginning riders at Smith Forks Campground, and a series of four-wheel-drive practice courses at Aliklik Campground.

On the east side of the SVRA, the Motocross Track, in the Quail Canyon Off-Road Event Area, is designed for use in competitive OHV events by organized groups and race promoters only, and is reservable. The primitive group camping area is there also, but may only be used for these special OHV events. Phone Hungry Valley SVRA for details.

The SVRA entrance is on Gold Hill Road at Peace Valley Road, on the SVRA's north side, near Gorman. A quarter mile south of this entrance, on Gold Hill Road, there is a registration and information booth. A ranger is present at times. This booth is near a day-use parking area with a vault toilet, dumpster, and pay phone.

Supplies, gasoline, and pay phones are available nearby in Gorman. An RV water station and dump station are located at Tejon Pass Rest Area, on I-5, north of Frazier Park.

For additional information, including special regulations and road conditions, write or phone Hungry Valley State Vehicular Recreation Area.

SITES, FACILITIES, RESTRICTIONS The SVRA contains nine camps with a total of over 140 individual sites for tents or RVs. These camps, on the west side of the SVRA, are listed separately in this book. The camps do not have piped drinking water or RV hookups. RVs must be self-contained (dump station: see above). The camps have dirt and gravel grounds with no lawns. Each site has a number on the side of its picnic shelter (ramada).

The SVRA is usually open. *Caution:* roads in Hungry Valley are crossed in several places by streams and creeks. Heavy rains bring flooding. Gold Hill Road and Hungry Valley Road are mostly paved but have some potholes and short stretches of dirt.

Camping limit is 14 days. No camping is permitted outside any camp. The speed limit is 15 m.p.h. within 15 feet of any camp. No wood may be gathered. Fires are permitted only in the camps' fire rings. Dogs must be leashed. The nightly fee is $1 per dog.

DIRECTIONS From Castaic, take I-5 north about 27 miles to the Gorman exit. Exit, turn left, and at Peace Valley Road, turn right (northwest). Go about a mile to the Hungry Valley SVRA entrance at Gold Hill Road (Forest Road 8N01). The sign mentions Hungry Valley SVRA but not Gold Hill Road. Turn left (south) to enter.

Edison Campground
Hungry Valley SVRA

GENERAL SETTING (LOCATION, FEATURES, SUPPLIES, INFORMATION) This camp, near the mouth of Edison Canyon, is the northernmost camp in the SVRA. The camping area is cleared of vegetation and has dirt-gravel grounds. A fenced OHV loading dock with ramp is at the north side of camp. Edison Canyon Trail, an OHV trail, leads east from camp into the low-lying oak hills. Roadrunner Trail, just east of camp, parallels Gold Hill Road.

For supplies, RV water and dump stations, the dog fee, and more information, see Hungry Valley SVRA, in this book.

SITES, FEES, FACILITIES, RESTRICTIONS The camp has 12 numbered sites for tents or RVs. The fee is $6 per site, per night.

Each site has a picnic table, a steel fire ring with grill, and a ramada (picnic shelter). Two vault toilets with wheelchair parking and access are near the entrance, along with a dumpster. The camp has several trash cans but no water or hookups.

The camp is usually open (closed during fires, floods, etc.). Camping limit is 14 days. For fires, use only the camp's fire rings.

DIRECTIONS Use directions for Hungry Valley SVRA, and continue on Gold Hill Road south about 2.2 miles to the camp's entrance on the left (east) side of the road.

Sterling Canyon Campground
Hungry Valley SVRA

GENERAL SETTING (LOCATION, FEATURES, SUPPLIES, INFORMATION) This camp is in the lower foothills, in a fairly open clearing with a few trees. Sterling Canyon Trail, near camp, leads west into the hills, along with other OHV trails. Across the road from camp, on the east side, is a trail through Big Canyon.

For supplies, RV water and dump stations, the dog fee, and more information, see Hungry Valley SVRA, in this book.

SITES, FEES, FACILITIES, RESTRICTIONS The camp has 12 numbered sites, of which 11 sites are for tents or RVs (no hookups); one site is for a tent only. The fee is $6 per site, per night.

Each site has a picnic table and a steel fire ring with grill. The tent site also has a bench and a Jeffrey pine tree for shade. Each of the other sites has a picnic shelter (ramada). Two wheelchair-accessible vault toilets are near the entrance. A bulletin board gives information about spark arresters. The camp has two dumpsters but no water. Three trash cans are placed on the far side of camp.

The camp is usually open (closed during fires, floods, etc.). Camping limit is 14 days. For fires, use only the camp's fire rings.

DIRECTIONS Use directions for Hungry Valley SVRA, and continue on Gold Hill Road south about 2.5 miles to the camp's entrance on the right (west) side of the road.

Circle Canyon Campground
Hungry Valley SVRA

GENERAL SETTING (LOCATION, FEATURES, SUPPLIES, INFORMATION) A glen of oak trees with cedar bushes, on the lower slope of a hill, makes an agreeable setting for this camp. This partly shady location, half a mile from the main road, distinguishes this camp from the others in Hungry Valley. Sites are arranged in a loop, or circle, as the camp's name implies. Approximately half the sites are at a lower level, as you enter the campground, and the other sites are up a little higher on the slope, with a view of the valley. The tall cedar bushes afford privacy at most sites, if not much shade.

About halfway along the side road to camp, you cross an OHV trail which leads to Red Tail Canyon, to the left (north). On the right (south) side of the road is a meeting place with a fire ring. For supplies, RV water and dump stations, the dog fee, and more information, see Hungry Valley SVRA, in this book.

SITES, FEES, FACILITIES, RESTRICTIONS The camp has 20 numbered sites for tents or RVs. The fee is $6 per site, per night.

Each site has a picnic table, a steel fire ring with grill, and a picnic shelter (ramada). Two vault toilets are located near the center of the camp loop, about halfway up between the lower and upper camping areas. A dumpster is provided, and sites share trash cans. The camp does not have water or hookups.

The camp is usually open (closed during fires, floods, etc.). Camping limit is 14 days. For fires, use only the camp's fire rings.

DIRECTIONS Use directions for Hungry Valley SVRA, and continue on Gold Hill Road south about 2.8 miles to the camp's entrance road. Turn left, and go about half a mile to camp (passing the "meeting place" with fire ring at about a quarter of a mile).

Cottonwood Campground
Hungry Valley SVRA

GENERAL SETTING (LOCATION, FEATURES, SUPPLIES, INFORMATION) This camp is set in a wide place at the mouth of a canyon, on Old Cottonwood Trail, a quarter mile from the main road. There are two camping areas, one at the front of camp, and the other at the rear. Cedar bushes afford privacy. Old Cottonwood Trail continues west of camp into the hills, as an OHV trail.

For supplies, RV water and dump stations, the dog fee, and more information, see Hungry Valley SVRA, in this book.

SITES, FEES, FACILITIES, RESTRICTIONS Of the camp's 14 numbered sites for tents or RVs, eight sites are at the front of camp and 6 sites are at the rear. The fee is $6 per site, per night.

Each site has a table, a steel fire ring with grill, and a picnic shelter (ramada). Two vault toilets and a dumpster can be found between the front and rear camping sections. Another dumpster is at the rear of camp. The camp has no water or hookups.

The camp is usually open (closed during fires, floods, etc.). *Caution:* two streams cross Gold Hill Road between Circle Canyon Camp, to the north, and this camp. The road is flooded during storms. Camping limit is 14 days. Fires are permitted only in the camp's fire rings.

DIRECTIONS Use directions for Hungry Valley SVRA, and continue on Gold Hill Road south about 3 miles to Old Cottonwood Trail. Turn right (west) and go about a quarter mile to camp.

Upper Scrub Oaks Campground
Lower Scrub Oaks Campground
Hungry Valley SVRA

GENERAL SETTING (LOCATION, FEATURES, SUPPLIES, IN-FORMATION) These camps are located very close to each other, just off the main road. In fact, four sites at the south end of Upper Scrub Oaks Camp are connected to Lower Scrub Oaks Camp by a very bumpy trail which parallels, and is close to, the main road. The camps are named for the majestic trees that are common here.

Upper Scrub Oaks Camp sits on a slight incline, on the lower slope of a foothill and has a nice view of Hungry Valley and Gold Hill Road. Campsites are placed in coves of cedar bushes and have some privacy. An OHV trail leads west from camp into the canyon.

Lower Scrub Oaks Camp is set at the base of a small rise. A large oak tree, with a fence around it, guards the entrance to camp. Flying W Trail is across the road from camp and leads east.

For supplies, RV water and dump stations, the dog fee, and more information, see Hungry Valley SVRA, in this book.

SITES, FEES, FACILITIES, RESTRICTIONS Upper Scrub Oaks Camp has 16 numbered sites for tents or RVs, plus a wheelchair-accessible site (near the toilets). Lower Scrub Oaks Camp has eight numbered sites for tents or RVs. The nightly fee is $6 per site.

At both camps, each campsite has a picnic table, a steel fire ring with grill, and a picnic shelter (ramada). Each camp has two vault toilets, with wheelchair parking and access, and a dumpster and some trash cans. Neither camp has water or hookups.

The camp is usually open (closed during fires, floods, etc.). Camping limit is 14 days. For fires, use only the camp's fire rings.

DIRECTIONS Use directions for Hungry Valley SVRA, and continue on Gold Hill Road south about 3.5 miles to Upper Scrub Oaks Camp. Go about half a mile farther to Lower Scrub Oaks Camp. Both camps are on the right (west) side of the road.

Smith Forks Campground
Hungry Valley SVRA

GENERAL SETTING (LOCATION, FEATURES, SUPPLIES, INFORMATION) This campground was placed at the main crossroads within Hungry Valley SVRA, where Gold Hill Road meets

Hungry Valley Road. The camp is in the middle of an open, desert-like plain, and is bare of foliage, except for some short cedar trees bordering sites along the north side, and some sagebrush just outside camp. Maxey Campground in this neighborhood was closed.

A fenced mini-track for motorcycles is located near the front of camp. Per the sign, only motorcycles under 90 c.c. are permitted and must be driven on the track in a counterclockwise direction. A fenced OHV loading dock with ramp is provided at the center of camp. Three unnumbered, day-use picnic sites are adjacent to the mini-track, at the front of camp (picnic facilities: see below).

For supplies, RV water and dump stations, the dog fee, and more information, see Hungry Valley SVRA, in this book.

SITES, FEES, FACILITIES, RESTRICTIONS There are 20 numbered sites for tents or RVs. The fee is $6 per site, per night.

Each campsite and each picnic site has a picnic table, a steel fire ring with grill, and a picnic shelter (ramada). Four vault toilets are provided, two at the front and two at the rear. The rear toilets are wheelchair accessible. The camp has two dumpsters and several trash cans. The camp has no water or hookups.

The camp is usually open (closed during fires, floods, etc.). Camping limit is 14 days. For fires, use only the camp's fire rings.

DIRECTIONS Use directions for Hungry Valley SVRA, and continue on Gold Hill Road south about 5 miles to the camp's entrance road. Turn left (east) and go about a tenth mile to camp.

Aliklik Campground
Hungry Valley SVRA

GENERAL SETTING (LOCATION, FEATURES, SUPPLIES, INFORMATION) The Four-Wheel-Drive Practice and Safety Training Area, next door to this camp, is a major attraction for OHV enthusiasts. There are all sorts of OHV courses to pick from here: Sluice Box, Sand Pit, Water Trough, Wheel Blocks, Hard Ditch, Stairsteps, and Boulder Climb. Adjacent to this section is a group picnic area with eight picnic tables and trash cans.

A fenced OHV loading dock with ramp is also provided. The campground is set in an open, barren, desert-like valley, and sites are placed by big cedar bushes that are almost the size of trees.

For supplies, RV water and dump stations, the dog fee, and more information, see Hungry Valley SVRA, in this book.

SITES, FEES, FACILITIES, RESTRICTIONS The camp has 15 numbered sites for tents or RVs. The fee is $6 per site, per night.

Each site has a picnic table, a steel fire ring with grill, and a picnic shelter. The camp has two vault toilets with wheelchair parking and access, a dumpster, trash cans, and a bulletin board with information on vehicle spark arresters, but no water or hookups.

The camp is usually open (closed during fires, floods, etc.). Camping limit is 14 days. For fires, use only the camp's fire rings.

DIRECTIONS Use directions for Hungry Valley SVRA, and continue on Gold Hill Road south about 5 miles to Hungry Valley Road. Turn left (east) and go about 0.75 mile to camp.

Lane Ranch Campground
Hungry Valley SVRA

GENERAL SETTING (LOCATION, FEATURES, SUPPLIES, INFORMATION) Shade trees provide this camp with a different atmosphere than other camps in Hungry Valley. This camp lies in a flat plain, away from the hills, and has an OHV loading dock with ramp. For supplies, RV water and dump stations, the dog fee, and more information, see Hungry Valley SVRA, in this book.

SITES, FEES, FACILITIES, RESTRICTIONS There are 25 numbered sites for tents or RVs (no hookups). There is also a wheelchair-accessible campsite. The fee is $6 per site, per night.

Each site has a picnic table, a steel fire ring with grill, and a picnic shelter (ramada). The camp has two vault toilets with wheelchair access, dumpsters, and trash cans, but no water.

The camp is usually open (closed during fires, floods, etc.). Camping limit is 14 days. For fires, use only the camp's fire rings.

DIRECTIONS Use directions for Hungry Valley SVRA, and continue on Gold Hill Road south about 5 miles to Hungry Valley Road. Turn left (east) and go about 2 miles to camp.

Kings and Gold Hill Campgrounds
U.S. Forest Service

GENERAL SETTING (LOCATION, FEATURES, SUPPLIES, INFORMATION) These very primitive camps have only fire rings at this time. The camps are located west of, and reached through, Hungry Valley State Vehicular Recreation Area. The elevation is

4200 feet at Kings Camp and 3800 feet at Gold Hill Camp. The two camps are less than a mile apart, but in different settings.

Kings Camp is about halfway along a canyon of pinyon pines, with tent sites on a shaded slope to the left (north) and RV sites in a shaded glen on the right (south). Trees scarred by a forest fire are seen along the side road leading to camp.

Gold Hill Camp has widely scattered tent sites. The camp sits on a cliff, within a canyon, high above Piru Creek. The camping area is mainly out in the open. Some sites are partly shaded by pinyon trees that border the sites and line the edge of the cliff. Piru Creek offers seasonal fishing (license required).

Purchase supplies and gasoline in Gorman, about 10 miles north, before making the long trip to the camps.

For more information, write or phone the Mount Pinos Ranger District of the Los Padres National Forest.

SITES, FEES, FACILITIES, RESTRICTIONS Kings Camp has six dirt sites, of which three are for tents only, and three are for tents or RVs (no hookups). Gold Hill Camp has seven dirt sites for tents only. At both camps, each site is nonreservable and takes up to eight people. A parked vehicle requires an Adventure Pass (fee).

At both camps, each site has a steel fire ring with grill. There are no tables, toilets, water, or other facilities (as of this writing). Portable toilets may be available at times; phone for updates. RV water and dump stations are available at Tejon Pass Rest Area, on I-5, north of Frazier Park (about 13 miles north of the camps).

These campgrounds are usually open, but are subject to closure during rains or fires. *Caution:* roads in this area are crossed by creeks, and become flooded during storms. The road to Gold Hill Camp is recommended for four-wheel-drive vehicles, because it is narrow, very bumpy, and has washboard stretches. Camping limit is 14 days. Maximum RV length at Kings Camp is 16 feet. Fires are restricted to the camps' fire rings. Dogs must be leashed.

DIRECTIONS Use directions for Hungry Valley SVRA, and continue on Gold Hill Road south about 10.5 miles, passing through Hungry Valley. At Forest Road 70N0A, turn left (east) and go about 0.75 mile to Kings Camp (no camp sign). Continue south on Gold Hill Road 0.25 mile to a short, dirt road. Turn right (west) and go about half a mile to Gold Hill Camp (no camp sign). Tent sites are scattered to the left (south), up and down the narrow dirt trails.

Dutchman Campground
Twin Pines Campground
U.S. Forest Service

GENERAL SETTING (LOCATION, FEATURES, INFORMA-TION, SUPPLIES) These small and very primitive tent camps are located on Alamo Mountain. The elevation is 6800 feet at Dutchman Camp and is 6600 feet at Twin Pines Camp. Both campgrounds are located west of, and reached through, Hungry Valley State Vehicular Recreation Area. The camps are partially shaded by Jeffrey pine trees.

Purchase supplies and gasoline in Gorman, about 20 miles north, before making the long trip to these campgrounds.

For more information, write or phone the Mount Pinos Ranger District of the Los Padres National Forest.

SITES, FEES, FACILITIES, RESTRICTIONS Dutchman Camp has eight tent sites, and Twin Pines Camp has five tent sites. Up to eight people are allowed per site. A parked vehicle requires an Adventure Pass (fee). All sites are of dirt and are nonreservable.

Each camp has fire rings, and Twin Pines Camp has a vault toilet (per the U.S. Forest Service). Neither campground has any water (bring your own).

Note: local dirt access roads were closed temporarily, due to repairs, at the time of this writing, so facility information was not verifiable on site. The camps are open otherwise from May to September, but are subject to closure during rains or fires. *Caution:* poor dirt roads, of about 5 miles in length, access these camps, so four-wheel-drive vehicles are recommended, but not trailers or motorhomes.

Camping limit is 14 days. No fires are permitted except in the campgrounds' fire rings. Dogs must be leashed.

DIRECTIONS Use directions for Hungry Valley SVRA, and continue on Gold Hill Road south about 17.5 miles, passing through Hungry Valley State Vehicular Recreation Area. The paved portion ends beyond Gold Hill Camp. At unpaved Alamo Mountain Road, turn right (west) and go a short distance to Twin Pines Camp, accessed on the left (south). Continue on Alamo Mountain Road for about 2 miles. The road bends south, and Dutchman Camp is accessed on the right (west).

Los Alamos Campground
Los Alamos Group Camp
Angeles National Forest

GENERAL SETTING (LOCATION, FEATURES, SUPPLIES, IN-FORMATION) These campgrounds are located between Castaic and Gorman, just a few miles northwest of the popular Pyramid Lake Recreation Area. Though the camps are located in Los Angeles County, they are included here because they are close to Ventura County. The camps and Pyramid Lake Recreation Area are on national forest land and are run by the same concessionaire. The camps are spread over a low rise at the edge of the foothills, with a view of the valley. The view of I-5 in the distance, to the east, is a reminder that civilization is not so far away, after all.

Individual campsites, at Los Alamos Campground, are divided into three loops, each of which is set in a short box canyon. These sites each have one tree or are unshaded. Los Alamos Group Camp's three sites are unshaded, although two sites are near trees. Camping is permitted only at the two campgrounds, not at Pyramid Lake Recreation Area, which is a day-use area only.

Pyramid Lake Recreation Area offers water-skiing, jet skiing, rental boating, and fishing for bass and catfish (license required). Swimming is allowed only at the swimming beach, open in summer only, with lifeguard service. For swimming fees, see below. There are several picnic areas; some are near parking lots and have wheelchair access; others, across the lake, can be reached only by boat, and have docks. Picnic area facilities include picnic tables, fire grills, shelters (ramadas), and flush toilets.

Pyramid Lake Marina features a snack bar, a general store with bait and tackle, boat rentals, a dock, and a boat ramp.

Supplies are available in Gorman, about 12 miles north of camp, via I-5, and in Castaic, about 18 miles south, via I-5. The camp office's store, at the camp entrance, has limited supplies. Los Alamos USFS Fire Station is about a mile west of camp.

For campground information and Pyramid Lake boating regulations, phone the concessionaire, or contact the Santa Clara/Mojave Rivers Ranger District of the Angeles National Forest.

SITES, FEES, FACILITIES, RESTRICTIONS Los Alamos Campground has 93 individual, nonreservable, numbered sites, among three loops, for tents or RVs, with gravel spurs (no hookups). The fee is $10 per site, per night. A limit of eight people and two vehicles per site is allowed. There is also a $5 fee for an extra vehicle. Some sites are paved and have wheelchair access, as do restrooms. Each individual site has a picnic table and a steel fire ring with grill. The three loops have water spigots, restrooms with sinks and RV-style flush toilets, and trash dumpsters, but no hookups.

Los Alamos Group Camp is large enough for 75 people. There are three group campsites, identified by letters (A, B, and C), for tents or RVs. The fee is $50 per group site, per night. Group reservations are required (phone for information). Los Alamos Group Camp is about half a mile west of Los Alamos Campground, and has its own entrance from the main road. Site A has no trees.

Each group site has a few picnic tables, a water spigot, a concrete fire ring without grill, and a pedestal barbecue or a steel fire ring with grill. There is a dumpster, a parking area, an outdoor laundry sink, and a restroom with sinks and pedal-flush toilets.

For registered campers, an RV dump station is provided near the camp office. A pay phone is available at the camp office.

Los Alamos Camp's Loop 2 and Los Alamos Group Camp are usually open (closed during fires, heavy rains, etc.). Loops 1 and 3 are open from Memorial Day weekend to Labor Day weekend. Camping limit is 14 days. Quiet hours are from 10 P.M. to 6 A.M. Maximum RV length is 32 feet. Fires are permitted only in the camps' fire rings and barbecues. Dogs must be leashed.

Pyramid Lake Recreation Area is open every day, 6 A.M. to 8 P.M. in summer, and 7 A.M. to 5 P.M. the rest of the year. The day-use parking fee is $6 per single vehicle, and $12 per vehicle with trailer. Swimming fees are $1 per adult and 50¢ per child. Fires are permitted at Pyramid Lake only in the picnic areas' barbecues.

DIRECTIONS From Castaic, take I-5 north about 18.5 miles to Smokey Bear Road. Exit and turn left (west), then at Pyramid Lake Road, turn left (south). Go about 1.5 miles to Emigrant Landing and a crossroad (no street name shown on sign). Turn right, drive over the bridge, and go about 2 miles to Los Alamos Campground, then about half a mile to Los Alamos Group Camp. Both camps are on the left (south) side of the road.

To reach Pyramid Lake, do not turn at Emigrant Landing, but continue straight ahead, on Pyramid Lake Road, to the entrance.

Hardluck Campground
U.S. Forest Service

GENERAL SETTING (LOCATION, RECREATION, SUPPLIES, INFORMATION) This primitive camp is located southwest of two fun-filled attractions, Pyramid Lake Recreation Area with marine recreation and fishing (license required), and Hungry Valley SVRA for OHV enthusiasts. For more information, see Los Alamos Campground and Hungry Valley SVRA, in this book.

The camp's elevation is 2800 feet. For hikers, nearby Buck Creek Trail (18W01) wanders into the Sespe Wilderness—a pleasant, wooded area of Douglas firs.

Los Alamos Fire Station (under U.S. Forest Service) is about 3 miles east of camp. Supplies are available in Gorman.

For more information, write or phone the Mount Pinos Ranger District of the Los Padres National Forest.

SITES, FEES, FACILITIES, RESTRICTIONS The camp has 22 nonreservable dirt sites for tents or RVs (no hookups). The nightly fee is $8 per site. Up to eight people are allowed at each site.

Facilities include picnic tables, fire rings, and vault toilets (per the U.S. Forest Service). An RV water station and dump station are located at Tejon Pass Rest Area, on I-5, north of Frazier Park.

Note: this camp has been temporarily closed for the protection of endangered species. Hardluck Road and Hardluck Camp were closed at the time of this writing, so facility information was not verifiable on site. The camp is usually open otherwise from April to November, but is subject to closure during fires and rains. Caution is advised on Hardluck Road, especially during rainy weather, since portions are unpaved.

Camping limit is 14 days. Maximum RV length is 22 feet. Fires are restricted to the camp's fire rings. Dogs must be leashed.

DIRECTIONS Use directions for Los Alamos Campground but continue west about 0.75 mile to a fork in the road. (Los Alamos Forest Station is to the left, south.) Bear to the right, heading straight ahead, on Hardluck Road; portions are unpaved. Go about 3 miles to the end of the road and Hardluck Campground.

Appendix 1
Directory

California State Parks and State Beaches

Reservations .... (800) 444-7275
California Department of Parks and Recreation .... (916) 653-6995
    Box 942896, Sacramento, CA 94296-0001
Carpinteria State Beach .... (805) 684-2811
    c/o Channel Coast District, 1933 Cliff Drive,
    Suite 27, Santa Barbara, CA 93109 .... (805) 899-1400
       Recorded information .... (805) 968-1033
El Capitan, Gaviota, and Refugio State Beaches ...... (805) 899-1400
    10 Refugio Beach Road, Goleta, CA 93117 .... (805) 968-1033
Emma Wood State Beach – Recorded information ..... (805) 968-1033
    c/o Channel Coast District, 1933 Cliff Drive,
    Suite 27, Santa Barbara, CA 93109
       North Beach Camp .... (805) 648-4807
       Ventura River Group Camp and
       San Buenaventura State Beach (Day-use) ...... (805) 648-4127
Hungry Valley State Vehicular Recreation Area .... (661) 248-7007
    Box 1360, Lebec, CA 93243-1360
       Motocross Track reservations .... (661) 294-0020
Leo Carrillo and Point Mugu State Beaches .... (805) 488-5223
    c/o Angeles District, 1925 Las Virgenes Road,
    Calabasas, CA 91302 .... (805) 488-1827
    Or .... (818) 880-0350
McGrath State Beach .... (805) 654-4744
    c/o Channel Coast District, 1933 Cliff Drive,
    Suite 27, Santa Barbara, CA 93109 .... (805) 648-4127
       Recorded information .... (805) 968-1033
       Special group events...................... (805) 648-4059

County Parks

Santa Barbara County Parks Department .... (805) 568-2461
    610 Mission Canyon Road, Santa Barbara, CA 93105
       Jalama Beach County Park .... (805) 736-3504
          Recorded information .... (805) 736-6316
          Group reservations .... (805) 934-6211
       Cachuma Lake Recreation Area .... (805) 686-5055
          Recorded information .... (805) 686-5054
          Reservations for groups, yurts, boat cruises .. (805) 686-5050
Ventura County Parks........................... (805) 654-3951
    800 South Victoria Avenue, Ventura, CA 93009-1030

U.S. Forest Service
Reservations . . . . (877) 444-6777
(except Paradise Camp, Sage Hill and Los Alamos Group Camps)

Los Padres National Forest Headquarters . . . . (805) 683-6711
6144 Calle Real, Goleta, CA 93117
Mount Pinos Ranger District . . . . (661) 245-3731
34580 Lockwood Valley Road, Frazier Park, CA 93225
McGill Camp and Group Camp, Mount Pinos Camp
Concessionaire . . . . (661) 248-6575
Ojai Ranger District . . . . (805) 646-4348
1190 East Ojai Avenue, Ojai, CA 93023
Wheeler Gorge Camp and Holiday Group Camp
Camp host . . . . (805) 640-1977
Concessionaire . . . . (805) 967-8766
Santa Barbara Ranger District . . . . (805) 967-3481
3505 Paradise Road, Santa Barbara, CA 93105
Fremont, Paradise, Los Prietos, Upper Oso Camps
Concessionaire . . . . (805) 967-8766
Paradise Camp, Sage Hill Group Camp
Reservations . . . . (877) 416-6992
Santa Lucia Ranger District . . . . (805) 925-9538
1616 North Carlotti Drive, Santa Maria, CA 93454

Angeles National Forest
Santa Clara/Mojave Rivers Ranger District . . . . (661) 296-9710
30800 Bouquet Canyon Road, Saugus, CA 91350
Los Alamos Camp and Group Camp, Pyramid Lake
Concessionaire and group reservations . . . . . . (661) 248-6575

Other Jurisdictions
Lake Casitas Recreation Area . . . . (805) 649-2233
11311 Santa Ana Road, Ventura, CA 93001
Reservations . . . . (805) 649-1122
Lake Piru Recreation Area . . . . (805) 521-1500
Box 202, Piru, CA 93040
Reservations . . . . (805) 521-1572
Mil Potrero Park
West Side Recreation and Park District . . . . (661) 763-4246
500 Cascade Place, Taft, CA 93268
River Park
Lompoc Parks and Recreation Department . . . . (805) 736-6565
125 West Walnut Avenue, Lompoc, CA 93436-6749

Critter Safety
Big Bear Discovery Center, Big Bear Ranger District . . . (909) 866-3437
Box 290, Fawnskin, CA 92333

California Department of Fish and Game . . . . (310) 590-5132
 330 Golden Shore, Suite 50, Long Beach, CA 90802
Cooperative Extension, UCSD . . . . (800) 200-2337
 UC Cooperative Extension–AHB,
 555 Overland Avenue, Building 4, San Diego, CA 92123
Trabuco Ranger District, Cleveland National Forest . . . (909) 736-1811
 1147 East 6th Street, Corona, CA 91719-1616

 # Appendix 2
Adventure Pass
U.S. Forest Service

 Those who visit Los Padres and Angeles National Forests for recreation must display an Adventure Pass on a parked vehicle. Recreation includes camping, picnicking, hiking, bicycling, horseback riding, swimming, surfing, skiing, fishing, hunting, and other activities. A day pass costs $5. A year pass costs $30 (good until December 31). The fine is $100 for not displaying a pass. A pass is not required at sites where camping or day-use fees are already charged. For clarification and more information, contact the local U.S. Forest Service offices. The pass may be purchased at those offices and at many sporting goods stores.

Appendix 3
Critters

 Usually the only creatures, other than humans, that may annoy campers are flies and mosquitos. While the probability of being struck by lightning is greater than being attacked by a mountain lion or bear, it is well to be aware that such creatures do exist in California's mountainous areas. The brochures listed below present information concerning these creatures and Africanized bees, and some precautions campers might take.

"Bear Us in Mind," Big Bear Discovery Center, Big Bear Ranger District, San Bernardino National Forest.
"Bee Alert: Africanized Honey Bee Facts," Cooperative Extension, University of California, San Diego.
"Living With California Bears," California Department of Fish and Game.
"Living With Mountain Lions," California Department of Fish and Game. Please report any close encounters with mountain lions, any attacks, and any sightings of dead or injured mountain lions to the California Department of Fish and Game.
"Mountain Lion Territory," Trabuco Ranger District, Cleveland National Forest.

Index

117